"*The Meditative Mind* is one of those unique books that is enjoyable reading and yields important, practical benefits. It deserves widespread attention."

Herbert Benson, M.D.,
Associate Professor of Medicine,
Harvard Medical School

"Goleman's book serves as an essential guide through the labyrinth of spiritual traditions. It is a valuable resource for anyone seeking to understand the commonality of different meditative disciplines, as well as their distinctions."

Joseph Goldstein,
author of *The Experience of Insight*

"*The Meditative Mind* is a scholarly yet thoroughly engaging and readable map of the world's great meditative traditions and their intersection with different religions and psychologies. A treasure trove of information and inspiration, this book is bound to become a classic."

Joan Borysenko, Ph.D.,
Instructor of Medicine, Harvard Medical School
Author of *Minding the Body, Mending the Mind*

THE
MEDITATIVE
MIND

Also by Daniel Goleman:

Vital Lies, Simple Truths:
  The Psychology of Self Deception

THE
MEDITATIVE
MIND

The Varieties of
Meditative Experience

DANIEL GOLEMAN
Foreword by Ram Dass

A Jeremy P. Tarcher/Putnam Book
published by
G. P. Putnam's Sons
New York

A Jeremy P. Tarcher/Putnam Book
Published by G. P. Putnam's Sons
Publishers Since 1838
200 Madison Avenue
New York, NY 10016
http://www.putnam.com/putnam

Library of Congress Cataloging-in-Publication Data

Goleman, Daniel.
    The meditative mind: varieties of meditative experience/Daniel Goleman.
        p.   cm.
    Updated ed. of: The varieties of the meditative experience. c1977.
    Bibliography.
    Includes index.
    ISBN 0-87477-833-6
    1. Meditation.   I. Goleman, Daniel. Varieties of the meditative experience.
II. Title.
BL627.G65   1988   87-29126   CIP
291.4'3—dc19

Printed in the United States of America
                6   7   8   9   10

To Neemkaroli Baba and Sayadaw U Pandita,
for Tara, Govinddas, and Hanuman

CONTENTS

Foreword   ix
Preface   xvii
Introduction   xxi

Part One. The Visuddhimagga: A Map
                for Inner Space   1
    1. Preparation for Meditation   2
    2. The Path of Concentration   10
    3. The Path of Insight   20

Part Two. Meditation Paths: A Survey   39
    4. Hindu Bhakti   41
    5. Jewish Kabbalah   48
    6. Christian Hesychasm   52
    7. Sufism   59
    8. Transcendental Meditation   66
    9. Patanjali's Ashtanga Yoga   71
   10. Indian Tantra and Kundalini Yoga   77

11. Tibetan Buddhism 82
12. Zen 87
13. Gurdjieff's Fourth Way 92
14. Krishnamurti's Choiceless Awareness 97

Part Three. Meditation Paths:
Their Essential Unity 102
15. Preparation for Meditation 102
16. Attention 104
17. Seeing What You Believe 107
18. Altered States in Meditation 110

Part Four. The Psychology of Meditation 114
19. Abhidhamma: An Eastern Psychology 114
20. Psychology East and West 139
21. Meditation: Research and
Practical Applications 162

Bibliography 190
Suggested Readings 199
Index 201

FOREWORD

Swiftly arose and spread around me the peace and joy
and knowledge that passes all the art and argument of
the earth; and I know that the hand of God is the elder
hand of my own, and I know that the Spirit of God
is the eldest brother of my own . . .

—Walt Whitman
Leaves of Grass

I have been in that heaven the most illumined
By light from Him, and seen things which to utter
He who returns hath neither skill nor knowledge;
For as it nears the object of its yearning
Our intellect is overwhelmed so deeply
It can never retrace the path that it followed.
But whatsoever of the holy kingdom
Was in the power of memory to treasure
Will be my theme until the song is ended.

—Dante
Inferno

Most of us do not have quite such a vivid and compelling experience as did Dante or Whitman, yet you and I do have moments when we become disoriented in time and/or space; moments when we seem to be at the doorway to another state of being; moments when our own personal viewpoint seems trivial and we sense a greater intuitive harmony in the universe. Perhaps your experiences have come after becoming "lost" in a compelling film, book, piece of art or music, or church service; perhaps after a period of reverie near a brook, a mountain, or the ocean; possibly as the result of a high fever; at the moment of a traumatic event; through drugs or childbirth; from looking at the stars or falling in love. What is so provocative about these moments is that we are out of personal control, and yet all seems harmonious and all right.

In these experiences we sense, though usually cannot articulate, a more profound meaning to our lives. The *sine qua non* of these experiences is that they are not mediated by our intellect. Often, however, immediately after they pass, we return to our analytic minds and attempt to label what has happened. And there is where the trouble begins. Disputes about labels have led to incredible human misunderstandings, even culminating in religious wars. Once we have labeled our experiences, these labels take on power of their own through their association with profound moments and, in addition, they give our egos the security that we know what's what, that we are in control. Some labels treat the experiences as psychological apparition: "I was out of my mind," a "hallucination," a "dissociated state," "surfacing of the unconscious mind," "hysteria," "delusion." Other labels, focusing on the content, imply a mystical or spiritual event: "God came to me"; "I came into the spirit"; "I felt the Presence of Christ," or "a spirit guide"; "I understood the Tao," or "the Dharma," or "the Divine Law."

In 1961 I became involved in a labeling dispute. Having ingested psilocybin, I had the most profound experience of my life to date. The context was religio-mystical, and a spiritual label seemed appropriate. However, I was at the time a social science professor at Harvard, and thus was quite sympathetic to labels that implied that the chemical was a psychotomimetic—that is, it made you crazy. If the chemical didn't make me crazy, I suspected the labeling conflict (often within myself) would ultimately do so. Carl Jung describes the insanity of Richard Wilhelm, translator of the *I Ching,* to be the result of his attempt to incorporate two disparate cultures into his being simultaneously.

Outwardly, the battle revolved around the little psilocybin mushroom. The Mexican Curanderos labeled it *Teonanactyl*—the flesh of the Gods—useful for divinitory and mystical experiences. Humphry Osmond made the labeling a little more palatable for the Western mind by inventing the word *psychedelic,* meaning "mind manifesting." The psychiatric community's label of the same mushroom was "a psychotomimetic triptomine derivative," of interest only for the experimental induction of pseudoschizophrenic states. Using one labeling system, we were explorers into the mystical realms tried by Moses, Mohammed, Christ, and Buddha. According to the other, we were damn fools, driving ourselves insane.

There was an intuitive validity to the use of the spiritual metaphors. Corroboration for these interpretations came from obvious parallels between the immediate experiences with psychedelics and the mystic literature. I resolved the almost unbearable dissonance by shifting in the direction of a spiritual interpretation. For five years we attempted to find labels that would optimize the value of these experiences for mankind. The issue had significant implications for the politics of human consciousness. Using one set of metaphors, every state of mind not continuous with rational, normal, waking consciousness was to be treated as deviant—as a reflection of lack of adjustment. The other set of metaphors treated altered states of consciousness as rare and precious opportunities for humanity to delve into greater realms of its own potential awareness. As such, these experiences ought to be cultivated rather than suppressed, even if they create a threat to existing social institutions. By raising this issue we were following in the footsteps of William James who, in 1902, wrote of altered states of consciousness in *Varieties of Religious Experience:*

> No account of the universe in its totality can be final, which leaves these other forms of consciousness quite disregarded. How to regard them is the question, for they are so discontinuous with ordinary consciousness. Yet they may determine attitudes, though they cannot furnish formulas, and open a region though they fail to give a map. At any rate, they forbid a premature closing of our accounts with reality.

We came to appreciate the sophistication and sensitivity of Eastern systems of labeling altered states of consciousness. For approximately 4000 years Eastern religions had been evolving maps and charts for the terrain of inner exploration. We could understand some of these, while others were based on cultural perspectives too alien to our own to be useful. In 1967 I went to India because of the attraction of these maps and I wanted to find a way—or perhaps a teacher—through which I could utilize the maps more effectively. I hoped then to be able to stabilize these altered states of consciousness and integrate them with normal everyday life. None of us had been able to do so with psychedelics.

In India I met Neemkaroli Baba, who was far more than I could have hoped for. He lived in the state called sahaj samadhi, in which altered states of consciousness were an integral part of his life. In his presence one had the feeling of boundless space and timelessness, as well as vast love and compassion. Maharaji, as we called him, once ingested a huge dose of psychedelics and, to my complete surprise, nothing happened. If his awareness was not limited to any place, then there was nowhere to go, for he was already here, in all its possibilities.

Seeing one and being one are two different things—and I'd much rather be one than see one. The question was how to effect the transformation from whom I thought I was to whom or what Maharaji was or wasn't. I took everything that came out of Maharaji's mouth as specific instruction, although I wasn't capable of following all of them. But then it got more complicated because he gave conflicting instructions. Now I realized I was confronting a teacher, like a Zen koan, who was not effective so long as one remained bound to the rational. From where I was standing, in my rational, righteous, analytic mind, I couldn't get to where I thought I was going. What to do?

In the presence of Maharaji I experienced my heart opening and felt previously unexperienced waves of ever more consuming love. Perhaps this was the way—drowning in love. But my mind would not be quiet. The social scientist—that skeptic—was not to be drowned without a struggle. Using all the tools, including my sensual desire and intellect, as well as guilt and sense of responsibility, my ego structure fought back. For example, in the temples in which Maharaji stayed, there were statues of Hanuman, a monkey-God who had all power due to his total devotion to God. Hanuman is deeply loved and honored by Maharaji's devotees. I sat before an eight-foot cement statue of a monkey, painted red, and I sang to him and meditated upon him. Every now and then a voice would observe, "Ah, sitting worshiping a cement monkey idol. You've really gone over the edge." This was the inner battle, for which the Bhagavad Gita is a metaphor.

My Buddhist friends said that the problem was a matter of discipline of mind and, upon questioning, Maharaji affirmed that if you brought your mind to one-pointedness you would know God. Perhaps that was what I had to do. So I started to meditate in earnest. The devotional path allowed too much play of mind, and I had to get tough with myself. In 1971 I began serious meditation practice in Bodh Gaya, where Buddha had been enlightened. In a series of ten day courses I, along with about 100 Westerners, was gently guided into Theravadan Buddhist meditation techniques— the ultimate in simplicity of practice.

During this period I met Anagarika Munindra, a Therevadan teacher who seemed, in his almost transparent quality, to reflect the mindful, light equanimity to which the method pointed. I was exhilarated by my first tastes of a new deep tranquility. I asked to learn more, and he introduced me to the Visuddhimagga, part of Buddhism's scholastic tradition. Finally, I, a Western psychologist, was truly humbled intellectually. For I saw what *psyche logos* was really about. Here, in this one volume, was an exquisitely articulated and inclusive category system of mental conditions, plus a philosophy and method for extricating your awareness from the tyranny of your own mind. Here was the labeling system I had been looking for since 1961. It was amazingly free of value judgments and thus lent itself to serving as a way of comparing disparate metaphorical systems concerning altered consciousness. I drank the book like a fine brandy.

Though my intellect was delighted by the system underlying the practices, I found myself becoming dry and resis-

tant to the meditation itself. Was this an error in the way
I was practicing the method, or was it a clue that this form
of spiritual practice was not my way? I happily left Bodh
Gaya to fulfill a promise to attend a bhakti celebration and
also to find Maharaji, who was my Guru. You may ask why,
if Maharaji, a Hindu, is my Guru, I would go to study
Buddhist meditation in the first place—rather than stay with
him. Well, the answer was that he wouldn't let me stay with
him, and he continuously reiterated *"Sub Ek"* (all is one).
He spoke at length of Christ and Buddha, and then threw
me out. Therefore, when I was away from Maharaji, it did
not seem inconsistent to pursue other traditions. For in the
method of Guru, all the other methods fed the process of
purification that would allow me to merge with my beloved
Maharaji. To merge would be the end of the journey.

When I left Bodh Gaya I had arranged to spend the
summer with Munindra in Kosani, a small Himalayan village. At the last minute he could not come, so Dan Goleman
and I, and about twenty others, practiced a collection of
Buddhist, Hindu, and Christian methods during that summer. In the course of it, in conversation with Dan, I found
that he and I held much in common. We were both trained
as psychologists; both connected with Harvard; both had the
same Guru; and both had an appreciation of Buddhist theory
and meditation practice. He was struggling, as I had been,
to integrate these disparate parts of our lives.

There were important differences between Dan and me.
Among them was the fact that he was motivated to bring
what he could, from these experiences and practices, home
to the scientific community. I, on the other hand, had long
since left academia. Dan could do the intellectual task of
integration: provide a needed overview of spiritual paths
and the states of consciousness they traverse. As you will find
in this book, he has done just that.

This work is the beginning of a systematic foundation for appreciating the universality of the spiritual journey, similar to the philosophical foundation set forth by Aldous Huxley in his *Perennial Philosophy*. And, certainly, when we can recognize the commonalities, then we can honor the differences.

RAM DASS

Barre, Massachusetts

PREFACE

I wrote the first part of this book while living in a tiny Himalayan village during monsoon season, 1971. For the previous several months I had been studying with Indian yogis and swamis, Tibetan lamas, and southern Buddhist laymen and monks. Strange terms and concepts assailed me: "samadhi," "jhana," "turiya," "nirvana," and a host of others used by these teachers to explain their spiritual paths. Each path seemed to be in essence the same as every other path, but each had its own way of explaining how to travel it and what major landmarks to expect.

I was confused. Things first began to jell in my understanding, though, with a remark by Joseph Goldstein, a teacher of insight meditation, at Bodh Gaya. It's simple mathematics, he said: All meditation systems either aim for One or Zero—union with God or emptiness. The path to the One is through concentration on Him, to the Zero is insight into the voidness of one's mind. This was my first guideline for sorting out meditation techniques.

A month or two later I found myself sitting out the monsoon rains in that hilltop village. Five of us had come there to study with a meditation teacher during the rains. He never showed up. Instead, there came a steady trickle of Westerners, sent by my Guru, Neemkaroli Baba. By the end of monsoon season there had gathered thirty or forty Western pilgrims. Among them were students of virtually every major spiritual tradition: of the various kinds of Indian yogas, of different sects of Tibetan Buddhism, of Sufism, of Christian contemplation, of Zen, of Gurdjieff, of Krishnamurti, and of innumerable individual swamis, gurus, yogis, and babas. Each brought his or her own small treasure of favored books and his trove of private anecdotes. From these literary and personal sources, I sorted out for myself the main similarities and differences among all these meditation paths.

The writings that evolved into this book began as explanations to myself. I needed maps, and each of these traditions had its own to offer. At various times each of these maps has helped me find my way in meditation or made me feel safe in unfamiliar territory. None is complete of itself, for all of them together will fail to explain every facet of any one meditator's experience. Each of us has his own private road to follow, though for periods we may cover well-traveled paths. The maps included here are among the best traveled. These are popular routes but by no means define the whole terrain. This mental territory is mostly unmapped; each of us is an explorer.

Foremost among my debts in writing this book is to Neemkaroli Baba, who inspired me to take seriously my own path. My understanding owes much to conversations and encounters with Sayadaw U Pandita, Ram Dass, Anagarika Munindra, Chogyam Trungpa, Bhagavan Das, Ananda Mayee Ma, Kunu Rinpoche, Krishnamurti, S. N. Goenka, Swami Muktananda, Nyanaponika Mahathera, Bhikku Nyanajivako, Joseph Goldstein, Herbert Guenther, K. K. Sah, Father Theophane, Yogi Ramagyadas, Charles

Reeder, and many others who actively follow these paths themselves. The editors of the *Journal of Transpersonal Psychology* encouraged me to put my work into the form of articles, from which parts of this book are abridged. My travels in Asia were as a Harvard Predoctoral Fellow and then as a research training fellow of the Social Science Research Council.

The Meditative Mind includes much of the work written during the decade following my return from Asia. It draws on portions of articles that first appeared in *Theories of Personality* (Wiley) by Calvin Hall and Gardner Lindzey, ReVision, *Psychology Today,* the *American Journal of Psychotherapy,* the *Journal of Transpersonal Psychology,* and a report to the Institute for Noetic Sciences. My thinking in these writings was influenced by discussions with many others who are pursuing similar interests, including Richard Davidson, Gary Schwartz, David McClelland, David Shapiro, Herbert Benson, Daniel Brown, Jack Engler, Mark Epstein, Jon Kabat-Zinn, Kathleen Speeth, Mihalyi Csikzentmihalyi, Gerald Fogel, Roger Walsh, and, especially, my wife, Tara Bennett-Goleman.

To all those who have helped me, I am deeply grateful.

INTRODUCTION

Meditation was new to the West some fifteen years ago when I wrote *The Varieties of the Meditative Experience,* which forms the first three parts of this book. To be sure, Eastern teachers such as Yogananda and D. T. Suzuki had come to America much earlier and had gained followers here and there. But during the late 1960s and early 1970s there was a blossoming interest in meditation like none the West had witnessed before.

Caught up in that interest, I began meditating in college, and, as a graduate student in psychology, I traveled to Asia to study the meditative traditions in their original settings. Those of us who were drawn to the meditation teachings of the East were confronted by a panoply of techniques, schools, traditions, and lineages. Suddenly we heard talk of strange states of consciousness and exotic states of being— "samadhi" and "satori," Boddhisattvas and tulkus.

It was new and unfamiliar terrain to us. We needed a Baedeker, a traveler's guide to this topography of the spirit. I wrote *Varieties* as such a guide, an overview of the major meditative traditions that were then finding so many eager students. My goal was to render the exotic more familiar and to show the underlying commonalities among these traditions while respecting their differences.

Now, more than a decade later, things have changed. Meditation has infiltrated our culture. Millions of Americans have tried meditation, and many have incorporated it into their busy lives. Meditation is now a standard tool used in medicine, psychology, education, and self-development. In addition, there are many old hands who are now well into their second decade as meditators.

As these meditators have taken their places in the ranks of businesspeople, professionals, and academics, they have made meditation a part of the fabric of the culture. People meditate at work to enhance their effectiveness; psychotherapists and physicians teach it to their patients; and graduate students write theses about it. *The Meditative Mind* extends *Varieties,* tracking this emergence and the progress of meditation in the Western mainstream.

I remember the late Tibetan teacher Chogyam Trungpa telling me in 1974, "Buddhism will come to the West as a psychology." The concept that Buddhism—like the other great spiritual traditions of the world   contained a psychology at all was news to me then. Over the years, though, the budding relationship between Eastern and Western psychologies became a major topic in my writing.

In the years after *Varieties* was written, I published a range of articles on the encounters between Western culture and the meditative traditions of the East. The topics included descriptions of Eastern psychologies, the receptivity and resistance of Western psychologists to these Eastern viewpoints, and the role of meditation in psychotherapy, medicine, and consciousness research.

Several of these articles have been incorporated into Part Four of this book. The reader should note that any apparent differences in tone are due to the varying forums in which these writings first appeared. Additionally, in Part Four the format includes female examples.

The chapter on Abhidhamma was originally written for a college textbook on personality theory. In their formal training, most psychologists are never taught that the meditative practices of the East are the applied branch of ancient psychological theories, some of which are as well-wrought as the theories of modern times. This chapter was written to remedy that deficit.

The chapter on meditation and stress is taken from an article I wrote for *Psychology Today* and includes a short instruction on how to meditate. A note on meditation and psychotherapy was originally published in a journal for psychotherapists. My discussion of the politics of consciousness was transcribed from a lecture for publication in the *Journal of Transpersonal Psychology*. And my reflections on meditation and consciousness research were written as a position paper for a foundation.

These new chapters add a crucial balance to the book. *Varieties* described many meditative states that are relatively rarified; the added material in this edition discusses more everyday applications and implications of meditation—how it helps one deal with stress and how it can improve the quality of life in general.

Still, despite its practical uses, the true context of meditation is spiritual life. At their height, the states of consciousness described in the classic sources can lift one out of the small-mindedness bred by daily pursuits as well as transform ordinary awareness.

Such transcendental states seem to be the seeds of spiritual life, and they have been experienced by the founders and early followers of every world religion. Moses receiving the Ten Commandments, Jesus' forty-day vigil in the wilderness, Allah's desert visions, and Buddha's enlightenment under the Bo Tree all bespeak extraordinary states of consciousness.

All too often, religious institutions and theologies outlive the transmission of the original transcendental states that generated them. Without these living experiences, the institutions of religion become pointless, and their theologies appear empty. In my view, the modern crisis of established religions is caused by the scarcity of the personal experience of these transcendental states—the living spirit at the common core of all religions.

And that spirit unites the diversity of meditative forms. As an old Zen saying puts it: "From of old there were not two paths. Those who have arrived all walked the same road."

PART ONE

THE VISUDDHIMAGGA:
A MAP FOR INNER SPACE

The classical Buddhist *Abhidhamma* is probably the broadest and most detailed traditional psychology of states of consciousness. In the fifth century A.D., the monk Buddhaghosa summarized the portion of Abhidhamma about meditation into the *Visuddhimagga,* the "Path of Purification" (Nana-moli, 1976).* Buddhaghosa explains that the ultimate "purification" should be strictly understood as *nibbana* (sanskrit: *nirvana*), which is an altered state of consciousness.

The Visuddhimagga was for centuries part of an oral textbook of Buddhist philosophy and psychology that aspiring monks memorized verbatim. Because it is so detailed and complete, the Visuddhimagga gives us a comprehensive picture of a single viewpoint regarding meditation. As such, it will give a good background and basis of comparison for understanding other kinds of meditation, the subject matter of Part II. The Visuddhimagga begins with advice on the best surroundings and attitudes for meditation. It then describes the specific ways the meditator trains his attention and the landmarks he encounters in traversing the meditative

*References to these and other books mentioned in the text can be found in the Bibliography.

1

path to the nirvanic state. It ends with the psychological consequences for the meditator of his experience of nirvana.*

The Visuddhimagga is a traditional recipe book for meditation, but it does not necessarily tell us about the specific practices of contemporary Theravadan Buddhists. The progression it describes is an ideal type and as such need not conform to the experiences of any given person. But experienced meditators will most certainly recognize familiar landmarks here and there.

1. PREPARATION
FOR MEDITATION

Practice begins with *sila* (virtue or moral purity). This systematic cultivation of virtuous thought, word, and deed focuses the meditator's efforts for the alteration of consciousness in meditation. "Unvirtuous thoughts," for example, sexual fantasies or anger, lead to distractedness during meditation. They are a waste of time and energy for the serious meditator. Psychological purification means paring away distracting thoughts.

The purification process is one of three major divisions of training in the Buddhist schema, the other two being

*In addition to the excellent translation from the original Pali by Nanamoli Thera (1976), other contemporary commentaries on the Visuddhimagga consulted include: Bhikku Soma (1949), E. Conze (1956), Kalu Rimpoche (1974), Kashyap (1954), Lama Govinda (1969), Ledi Sayadaw (1965), Mahasi Sayadaw (1965, 1970), Narada Thera (1956), Nyanaponika Thera (1949, 1962, 1968), Nyanatiloka (1952a and b, 1972), P. V. Mahathera (1962).

samadhi (meditative concentration) and *puñña* (insight). Insight is understood in the special sense of "seeing things as they are." Purification, concentration, and insight are closely related. Efforts to purify the mind facilitate initial concentration, which enables sustained insight. By developing either concentration or insight, purity becomes, instead of an act of will, effortless and natural for the meditator. Insight reinforces purity, while aiding concentration; strong concentration can have as by-products both insight and purity. The interaction is not linear; the development of any one facilitates the other two. There is no necessary progression, rather a simultaneous spiral of these three in the course of the meditation path. Though the presentation here is of necessity linear, there is a complex interrelation in the meditator's development of purity, concentration, and insight. These are three facets of a single process.

Active purification in the Visuddhimagga tradition begins with the observance of codes of discipline for laity, novices, and fully ordained monks. The precepts for laity are but five: abstaining from killing, stealing, unlawful sexual intercourse, lying, and intoxicants. For novices the list expands to ten, the first five becoming stricter in the process. For monks there are 227 prohibitions and observances regulating every detail of daily monastic life. While the practice of purity varies with one's mode of life, its intent is the same: It is the necessary preparation for meditation.

On one level these are codes for proper social behavior, but that is secondary in importance to the motivational purity that proper behavior foreshadows. Purity is understood not only in the ordinary external sense of propriety but also as the mental attitudes out of which proper speech, action, and thought arise. Thus, for example, the Visuddhimagga urges the meditator, should lustful thoughts arise, immediately to counter those thoughts by contemplating the body in the aspect of loathsomeness. The object is to free the meditator from thoughts of remorse, guilt, or shame, as well as from lust. Behavior is controlled because it affects the mind. Acts of purity are meant to produce a calmed and subdued mind. The purity of morality has only the purity of mind as its goal.

Because a controlled mind is the goal of purity, restraint of the senses is part of purification. The means for this is *sati* (mindfulness). In mindfulness, control of the senses comes through cultivating the habit of simply noticing sensory perceptions, not allowing them to stimulate the mind into thought chains of reaction. Mindfulness is the attitude of paying sensory stimuli only the barest attention. When systematically developed into the practice of *vipassana* (seeing things as they are), mindfulness becomes the avenue to the nirvanic state. In daily practice, mindfulness leads to detachment toward the meditator's own perceptions and thoughts. He becomes an onlooker to his stream of consciousness, weakening the pull to normal mental activity and so preparing the way to altered states.

In the initial stages, before firm grounding in mindfulness, the meditator is distracted by his surroundings. The Visuddhimagga accordingly gives instructions to the would-be meditator for the optimum life-style and setting. He must engage in "right livelihood" so that the source of his financial support will not be cause for misgivings; in the case of monks, professions such as astrology, palm reading, and dream interpretation are expressly forbidden, while the life of a mendicant is recommended. Possessions should be kept to a minimum; a monk is to possess only eight articles: three robes, a belt, a begging bowl, a razor, a sewing needle, and sandals. He should take food in moderation, enough to ensure physical health but less than would make for drowsiness. His dwelling should be aloof from the world, a place of solitude; for householders who cannot live in isolation, a room should be set aside for meditation. Undue concern for the body should be avoided, but in case of sickness, the meditator should obtain appropriate medicine. In acquiring the four requisites of possessions, food, dwelling, and medicine, the meditator should get only what is necessary to his well-being. In getting these requisites, he should act without greed, so that even his material necessities will be untainted by impurity.

Since one's own state of mind is affected by the state of mind of one's associates, the serious meditator should surround himself with like-minded people. This is one advantage of *sanghas,* narrowly defined as those who have attained the nirvanic state and, in its widest sense, the community of people on the path. Meditation is helped by the company of mindful or concentrated persons and is harmed by those who are agitated, distracted, and immersed in worldly concerns. Agitated, worldly people are likely to talk in a way that does not lead to detachment, dispassion, or tranquility, qualities the meditator seeks to cultivate. The sort of topics typical of worldly, unprofitable talk are enumerated by the Buddha as (Nyanaponika Thera, 1962: p. 172)

about kings, thieves, ministers, armies, famine, and war; about eating, drinking, clothing and lodging; about garlands, perfumes, relatives, vehicles, cities and countries; about women and wine, the gossip of the street and well; about ancestors and various trifles; tales about the origin of the world, talk about things being so or otherwise, and similar matters.

At later stages, the meditator may find to be obstacles what once were aids. The Visuddhimagga lists ten categories of potential attachments, all hindrances to progress in meditation: (1) any fixed dwelling place if its upkeep is the cause of worry, (2) family, if their welfare causes concern, (3) accruing gifts or reputation that involves spending time with admirers, (4) a following of students or being busy with teaching, (5) projects, having "something to do," (6) traveling about, (7) people dear to one whose needs demand attention, (8) illness necessitating undergoing treatment, (9) theoretical studies unaccompanied by practice, and (10) supernormal psychic powers, the practice of which becomes more interesting than meditation. Release from these obligations frees the meditator for single-minded pursuit of meditation: This is "purification" in the sense of freeing the mind from worrisome matters. The life of the monk is designed for this kind of freedom; for the layman, short retreats allow a temporary reprieve.

These ascetic practices are optional in the "middle way" of the Buddha. The serious monk can practice them, should he find any of them helpful. But he must be discreet in their observance, doing them so that they will not attract undue attention. These practices include wearing only robes made of rags; eating only one bowl of food, and just once a day; living in the forest under a tree; dwelling in a cemetery or in the open; sitting up throughout the night. Though optional, the Buddha praises those who follow these modes of living "for the sake of frugality, contentedness, austerity, detachment," while criticizing those who pride themselves on practicing austerities and look down on others who do not. In all facets of training, spiritual pride mars purity. Any gains from asceticism are lost in pride. The goal of purification is simply a mind unconcerned with externals, calm and ripe for meditation.

Entering the Path of Concentration

Purity is the psychological base for concentration. The essence of concentration is nondistractedness; purification is the systematic pruning away of sources of distraction. Now the meditator's work is to attain unification of mind, one-pointedness. The stream of thought is normally random and scattered. The goal of concentration in meditation is to focus the thought flow by fixing the mind on a single object, the meditation topic. In the later stages of concentrative meditation, the mind is not only directed toward the object but finally penetrates it; totally absorbed in it, the mind moves to oneness with the object. When this happens, the object is the only thing in the meditator's awareness.

Any object of attention can be the subject for concentrative meditation, which is simply sustaining a single point of focus. But the character of the object attended to has definite consequences for the outcome of meditation. The Visuddhimagga recommends forty meditation subjects:

- ten *kasinas,* colored wheels about a foot in circumference: earth, water, fire, air, dark blue, yellow, blood-red, white, light, bounded space
- ten *asubhas,* loathsome, decaying corpses: for example, a bloated corpse, a gnawed corpse, a worm-infected corpse, etc., including a skeleton
- ten reflections: on the attributes of the Buddha, the Doctrine, the sangha, peace, one's own purity, one's own liberality, one's own possessions of godly qualities, or on the inevitability of death; contemplation on the thirty-two parts of the body or on in-and-out breathing
- four sublime states: loving-kindness, compassion, joy in the joy of others, and equanimity

- four formless contemplations: of infinite space, infinite consciousness, the realm of nothingness, and the realm of "neither perception nor non perception"; the loathsomeness of food
- the four physical elements: earth, air, fire, water as abstract forces (i.e., extension, motility, heat, cohesion)

Each of these subjects has specific consequences for the nature, depth, and by-products of concentration; meditation on a corpse, for example, becomes very different from contemplating loving-kindness. All of these subjects are suitable for developing concentration to the depth necessary for attaining the nirvanic state. The concentration produced by those of a complicated nature—for example, the attributes of the Buddha—is less unified than that produced by a simple object—for example, the earth kasina, a clay-colored wheel. Apart from the depth of concentration produced by a given meditation subject, each has distinct psychological by-products. The meditation on loving-kindness, for example, has several results: The meditator sleeps and wakes in comfort; he dreams no evil dreams; he is dear to all beings; his mind is easily concentrated; his expression is serene; and he dies unconfused.

The Buddha saw that persons of different temperaments are more suited to some meditation subjects than to others. His guidelines for matching people to the best meditation subject is based on these main types of temperament: (1) one disposed to hatred; (2) the lustful, deluded, or excitable; (3) one prone to faith; (4) the intelligent.

Subjects suitable for the hateful type are: the four sublime states and the four color kasinas; for the lustful, the ten corpses, the body parts, and the breath; for the faithful, the first six reflections; and for the intelligent, reflection on death, the loathsomeness of food, and the physical elements. The remaining subjects are suitable for everyone. The Visuddhimagga also specifies the appropriate physical surrounding for each type. The lustful meditator, for example, should be assigned a cramped, windowless hut in an ugly location in the neighborhood of unfriendly people; the hateful type, on the other hand, is to be given a comfortable and roomy cottage in a pleasant area near helpful people.

The Teacher

The ideal meditation teacher was the Buddha, who, it is said, had developed the power to know the mind and heart of others. He perfectly matched each person with the appropriate subject and circumstance for concentration. In lieu of such an ideal teacher, the Visuddhimagga advises the would-be meditator to pick his* teacher according to level of attainment in meditation, the most highly accomplished being the best teacher. The teacher's support and advice are critical to the meditator in making his way through unfamiliar mental terrain. The pupil "takes refuge" in his teacher, entering a contract of surrender to him.

The pupil surrenders egoism, the source of hindrances that prevent him from pursuing meditation to the point at which egoism is transcended. But the responsibility for salvation is laid squarely on the student's own shoulders, not on the teacher's; the teacher is merely a "good friend" on the path. The teacher points the way; the student must walk for

---

*For "he" and "him" throughout Parts One through Three of this book, read "he/she" and "him/her." The path of meditation is clearly not closed to members of any sex, race, or creed.

himself. The essence of the teacher's role is given in the lines from the Japanese *Zenrin:*

If you wish to know the road up the mountain,
You must ask the man who goes back and forth on it.

2. THE PATH
OF CONCENTRATION

In describing the path of concentration, the Visuddhimagga map suffers from a serious oversight: It begins with the description of an advanced altered state, one that many or most meditators may never once experience. It skips the ordinary—and much more common—preliminary stages. This gap can be filled from other Buddhist sources, which start with the meditator's normal state of mind rather than with the rarefied states the Visuddhimagga elaborates in detail.

At the outset, the meditator's focus wanders from the object of meditation. As he notices he has wandered, he returns his awareness to the proper focus. His one-pointedness is occasional, coming in fits and starts. His mind oscillates between the object of meditation and distracting thoughts, feelings, and sensations. The first landmark in concentration comes when the meditator's mind is unaffected both by outer distractions, such as nearby sounds, and by the turbulence of his own assorted thoughts and feelings. Although sounds are heard, and his thoughts and feelings are noticed, they do not disturb the meditator.

In the next stage, his mind focuses on the object for prolonged periods. The meditator gets better at repeatedly returning his wandering mind to the object. His ability to return his attention gradually increases as the meditator sees the ill results of distractions (e.g., agitation) and feels the advantages of a calm one-pointedness. As this happens, the meditator is able to overcome mental habits antagonistic to calm collectedness, such as boredom due to hunger for novelty. By now, the meditator's mind can remain undistracted for long periods.

On the Verge of Absorption

In the early stages of meditation, there is a tension between concentration on the object of meditation and distracting thoughts. The main distractions are sensual desires; ill will, despair, and anger; laziness and torpor; agitation and worry; and doubt and skepticism. With much practice, a moment comes when these hindrances are wholly subdued. There is then a noticeable quickening of concentration. At this moment, the mental attributes, such as one-pointedness and bliss, that will mature into full absorption simultaneously come into dominance. Each has been present previously to different degrees, but when they come, all at once they have special power. This is the first noteworthy attainment in concentrative meditation; because it is the state verging on full absorption, it is called "access" concentration.

This state of concentration is like a child not yet able to stand steady but always trying to do so. The mental factors of full absorption are not strong at the access level; their emergence is precarious, and the mind fluctuates between them and its inner speech, the usual ruminations and wandering thoughts. The meditator is still open to his senses and remains aware of surrounding noises and his body's feelings. The meditation subject is a dominant thought but does not yet fully occupy the mind. At this access level, strong feelings of zest or rapture emerge, along with happiness, pleasure, and equanimity. There is also fleeting attention to the meditation subject as though striking at it, or more sustained focus on it, repeatedly noting it. Sometimes there are luminous shapes or flashes of bright light, especially if the meditation subject is a kasina or respiration. There may also be a sensation of lightness, as though the body were floating in the air. Access concentration is a precarious attainment. If not solidified into fuller absorption at the same sitting, it must be protected between sessions by avoiding distracting actions or encounters.

Visions

Visionary experiences can occur on the threshold of this level when factors such as rapture have ripened but discursive thought continues, and so long as sustained focus on the object of concentration remains weak. Were sustained concentration to achieve full strength, mental processes necessary for visions would be cut short as long as attention remains with the primary object. Access and deeper levels of absorption are for this reason antithetical to visions, but as the access level is approached (or on emerging from deeper absorption), visions are most likely. Visions can be frightening—an image of oneself as a corpse, for example, or the form of a threatening and terrifying beast—or quite benign, such as the figure of a benevolent deity or a Buddha. Meditative visions are quite vivid; the Visuddhimagga says they are as realistic as talking to a guest who comes on a visit. Timid or anxious persons who have a terrifying vision, it is warned, can be driven mad. Another danger to the meditator is becoming enraptured by beatific visions and so halting further progress by making them the goal of one's meditation, failing to further strengthen concentration. The meditator's goal is beyond visions. In Zen, they say, "If you meet the Buddha, slay him."

Full Absorptions or Jhana

By continually focusing on the object of meditation, there comes the first moment marking a total break with normal consciousness. This is full absorption, or *jhana*. The mind suddenly seems to sink into the object and remains fixed in it. Hindering thoughts cease totally. There is neither sensory perception nor the usual awareness of one's body; bodily pain cannot be felt. Apart from the initial and sustained attention to the primary object, consciousness is dominated by rapture, bliss, and one-pointedness. These are the mental factors that, when in simultaneous ascendance, constitute jhana.

There is a subtle distinction between rapture and bliss. Rapture at the level of the first jhana is likened to the initial pleasure and excitement of getting a long-sought object; bliss is the enjoyment of that object. Rapture may be experienced as raising of the hairs on the body, as momentary joy that flashes and disappears like lightning, as waves showering through the body again and again, as the sensation of levitation, or as immersion in thrilling happiness. Bliss is a more subdued state of continued ecstasy. One-pointedness is the property of mind that centers it in the jhanic state. The first taste of jhana lasts but a single moment, but with continued efforts, the jhanic state can be held for longer and longer intervals. Until the jhana is mastered, it is unstable and can be easily lost. Full mastery comes when the meditator can attain jhana whenever, wherever, as soon as, and for as long as he wishes.

Deeper Jhanas

In the course of meditation, one-pointedness becomes more and more intensified by the successive elimination of the jhanic factors. One-pointedness absorbs the energy invested in the other factors at each deeper jhanic level (Fig. 1). Becoming even more one-pointed after mastery of the first jhana requires eliminating initial and repeated returning of the mind to the meditation object. After emerging from the jhanic state, these attentional processes seem gross in comparison to the other more subtle mental factors of jhana. Just as the hindrances were overcome on the way to the access level, and just as thoughts were stilled in attaining the first jhana, initial and repeated attention to the primary object are abandoned at the threshold of the second jhana. To go beyond these kinds of attention, the meditator enters the first jhana by focusing on the primary object. But then he frees the mind of any thought of the object by instead turning the mind toward rapture, bliss, and one-pointedness. This level of absorption is more subtle and stable than the first. The meditator's mind is now totally free of any verbal thoughts, even that of the original primary object. Only a reflected image of the object remains as the focus of one-pointedness.

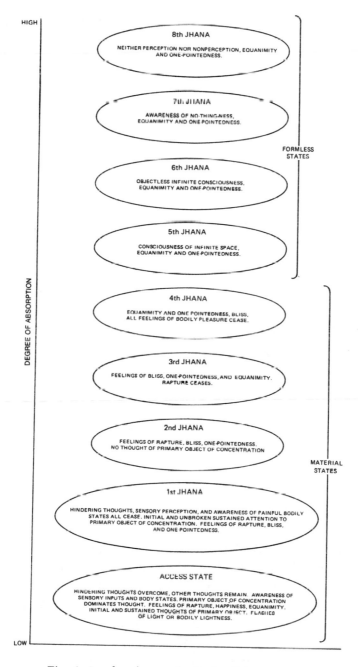

Fig. 1. Landmarks on the Path of Concentration.

Third Jhana

To go still deeper, the meditator masters the second jhana
as he did the first. Then, when he emerges from the second
jhana, he sees that rapture—a form of excitement—is gross
compared to bliss and one-pointedness. He attains the third
level of jhana by again contemplating the primary object
and abandoning first thoughts of the object, then rapture. In
the third level of absorption, there is a feeling of equanimity
toward even the highest rapture. This even-mindedness
emerges with the fading away of rapture. This jhana is
extremely subtle, and without this newly emergent equanimity, the meditator's mind would be pulled back to
rapture. If he stays in the third jhana, an exceedingly sweet
bliss fills the meditator, and afterward this bliss floods his
body. Because the bliss of this level is accompanied by
equanimity, the meditator's mind is kept one-pointed in
these subtle dimensions, resisting the pull of a grosser rapture. Having mastered the third jhana as those before, the
meditator can go deeper if he sees that bliss is more disturbing than one-pointedness and equanimity.

Fourth Jhana

To go deeper still, the meditator has to abandon all forms
of mental pleasure. He has to give up all those mental states
that might oppose more total stillness, even bliss and rapture.
With the total cessation of bliss, equanimity and one-pointedness gain their full strength. In the fourth jhana, feelings
of bodily pleasure are fully abandoned; feelings of pain
ceased at the first jhana. There is not a single sensation or
thought. The meditator's mind at this extremely subtle level

rests with one-pointedness in equanimity. Just as his mind becomes progressively more still at each level of absorption, his breath becomes calmer. At this fourth level, the meditator's breath is so still he cannot sense the least stirring; he perceives his breath as ceasing altogether.

Formless Jhana

The next step in concentration culminates in the four states called "formless." The first four jhanas are attained by concentration on a material form or some concept derived therefrom. But the meditator attains the formless states by passing beyond all perception of form. To enter the first four jhanas, the meditator had to empty his mind of mental factors. To enter each successive formless jhana, the meditator substitutes progressively more subtle objects of concentration. All the formless jhanas share the mental factors of one-pointedness and equanimity, but at each level these factors are more refined. Concentration approaches imperturbability. The meditator cannot be disturbed but emerges after a self-determined time limit set before entering this state.

Fifth Jhana

The meditator reaches the first formless absorption and the fifth jhana by entering the fourth jhana through any of the kasinas. Mentally extending the limits of the kasina to the largest extent imaginable, his attention is then turned away from the colored light of the kasina and toward the infinite space occupied by it. The meditator's mind now abides in a sphere in which all perceptions of form have ceased. With the full maturity of equanimity and one-pointedness, his mind is so firmly set in this sublime consciousness that nothing can disrupt it. Still, the barest trace of the senses exists in the fifth jhana, though they are ignored. The absorption would be broken should the meditator turn his attention to them.

Once the fifth jhana is mastered, the meditator goes still deeper by first achieving an awareness of infinite space and then turning his attention to that infinite awareness. In this way, the thought of infinite space is abandoned, while objectless infinite awareness remains. This marks the sixth jhana. Having mastered the sixth, the meditator obtains the seventh jhana by first entering the sixth and then turning his awareness to the nonexistence of infinite consciousness. Thus, the seventh jhana is absorption with no-thing-ness, or the void, as its object. That is, the meditator's mind takes as its object the awareness of absence of any object.

Mastering this seventh jhana, the meditator can then review it and find any perception at all a disadvantage, its absence being more sublime. So motivated, the meditator attains the eighth jhana by first entering the seventh. He then turns his attention to the aspect of peacefulness and away from perception of the void. The delicacy of this is suggested by the stipulation that there must be no hint of desire to attain this peacefulness or to avoid perception of no-thing-ness. Attending to the peacefulness, he reaches an ultrasubtle state in which there are only residual mental processes. There is no gross perception here at all: This is a state of "no perception." There *is* ultrasubtle perception: thus, "not nonperception." The eighth jhana, therefore, is called the "sphere of neither perception nor nonperception." No mental states are decisively present: Their residuals remain, though they are nearly absent. This state approaches the ultimate limits of perception. As with mind, so with body;

the meditator's metabolism becomes progressively stiller through the formless jhanas. "The eighth jhana," says one commentator, "is a state so extremely subtle that it cannot be said whether it is or is not."

Each jhana rests on the one below. In entering any jhana, the meditator's mind traverses upward each level in succession by eliminating the gross elements of each one by one. With practice, the traversal of jhanic levels becomes almost instantaneous, the meditator's awareness pausing at each level on the way for but a few moments of consciousness. As grosser mental factors are eliminated, concentration intensifies. The grossness of a meditation subject limits the depth of jhana the meditator can reach through it. The simpler the subject, the deeper the jhana (Table 1).

TABLE 1
JHANA LEVEL ATTAINABLE ACCORDING TO MEDITATION SUBJECT

Meditation Subject	*Highest Jhana Level Attainable*
Reflections; elements; loathsomeness of food	Access
Body parts; corpses	First
Loving-kindness; selfless joy; compassion	Third
Equanimity	Fourth
Infinite space	Fifth
Infinite consciousness	Sixth
No-thing-ness	Seventh
Kasinas; mindfulness of breath; neither perception nor nonperception	Eighth

3. THE PATH
OF INSIGHT

The Visuddhimagga sees mastery of the jhanas and tasting their sublime bliss as of secondary importance to puñña, discriminating wisdom. Jhana mastery is part of a fully rounded training, but its advantages for the meditator are in making his mind wieldy and pliable, so speeding his training in puñña. Indeed, the deeper jhanas are sometimes referred to in Pali, the language of the Visuddhimagga, as "concentration games," the play of well-advanced meditators. But the crux of his training is a path that need not include the jhanas. This path begins with mindfulness *(satipatthana),* proceeds through insight *(vipassana),* and ends in nirvana.

Mindfulness

The first phase, mindfulness, entails breaking through stereotyped perception. Our natural tendency is to become habituated to the world around us, no longer to notice the familiar. We also substitute abstract names or preconceptions for the raw evidence of our senses. In mindfulness, the meditator methodically faces the bare facts of his experience, seeing each event as though occurring for the first time. He does this by continuous attention to the first phase of perception, when his mind is *receptive* rather than reactive. He restricts his attention to the bare notice of his senses and thoughts. He attends to these as they arise in any of the five senses or in his mind, which, in the Visuddhimagga, constitutes a sixth sense. While attending to his sense impressions, the meditator keeps reaction simply to registering whatever he observes. If any further comment, judgment, or reflection arises in the meditator's mind, these are themselves made the focus of bare attention. They are neither repudiated nor pursued but simply dismissed after being noted. The essence of mindfulness is, in the words of Nyanaponika Thera, a modern Buddhist monk, "the clear and single-minded awareness of what actually happens *to* us and *in* us, at the successive moments of perception."

Whatever power of concentration the meditator has developed previously helps him in the thorough pursuit of mindfulness. One-pointedness is essential in adopting this new habit of bare perception. The best level of jhana for practicing mindfulness is the lowest, that of access. This is because mindfulness is applied to normal consciousness, and from the first jhana on, these normal processes cease. A level of concentration less than that of access, on the other hand, can be easily overshadowed by wandering thoughts and lapses in mindfulness. At the access level, there is a desirable balance: Perception and thought retain their usual patterns, but concentration is powerful enough to keep the meditator's awareness being diverted from steadily noting these patterns. The moments of entry to or exit from jhana are especially ripe for practicing insight. The mind's workings are transparent in these moments, making them more vulnerable to the clear gaze of the mindful meditator.

The preferred method for cultivating mindfulness is to precede it with training in the jhanas. There is, however, a method called "bare insight" in which the meditator begins mindfulness without any previous success in concentration. In bare insight, concentration strengthens through the practice of mindfulness itself. During the first stages of bare insight, the meditator's mind is intermittently interrupted by wandering thoughts between moments of mindful noticing. Sometimes the meditator notices the wandering, sometimes not. But momentary concentration gradually strengthens as more stray thoughts are noted. Wandering thoughts subside as soon as noticed, and the meditator resumes mindfulness immediately afterward. Finally, the meditator reaches the point at which his mind is unhindered by straying. When he notices every movement of the mind without break, this is the same as access concentration.

Kinds of Mindfulness

There are four kinds of mindfulness, identical in function but different in focus. Mindfulness can focus on the body, on feelings, on the mind, or on mind objects. Any one of these serves as a fixed point for bare attention to the stream of consciousness. In mindfulness of the body, the meditator attends to each moment of his bodily activity, such as his posture and the movements of his limbs. The meditator notes his body's motion and position regardless of what he does. The aims of his act are disregarded; the focus is on the bodily act itself. In mindfulness of feeling, the meditator focuses on his internal sensations, disregarding whether they are pleasant or unpleasant. He simply notes all his internal feelings as they come to his attention. Some feelings are the first reaction to messages from the senses, some are physical feelings accompanying psychological states, some are by-products of biological processes. Whatever the source, the feeling itself is registered.

In mindfulness of mental states, the meditator focuses on each state as it comes to awareness. Whatever mood, mode of thought, or psychological state presents itself, he simply registers it as such. If, for instance, there is anger at a disturbing noise, at that moment he simply notes "anger." The fourth technique, mindfulness of mind objects, is virtually the same as the one just described save for the level at which the mind's workings are observed. Rather than noting the quality of mental states as they arise, the meditator notes the attentional objects that occupy those states, for example, "disturbing noise." As each thought arises, the meditator notes it in terms of a detailed schema for classifying mental content. The broadest category on this list labels all thoughts as either hindrances to or helps toward enlightenment.

Any of these techniques of mindfulness will break through the illusions of continuity and reasonableness that sustain our mental life. In mindfulness, the meditator begins to witness the random units of mind stuff from which his reality is built. From these observations emerge a series of realizations about the nature of the mind. With these realizations, mindfulness matures into insight.

Beginning of Insight

The practice of insight begins at the point when mindfulness continues without lag. In insight meditation, awareness fixes on its object so that the contemplating mind and its object arise together in unbroken succession. This point marks the beginning of a chain of insights—mind knowing itself—ending in the nirvanic state (Fig. 2).

The first realization in insight is that the phenomena contemplated are distinct from mind contemplating them: Within the mind, the faculty whereby mind witnesses its own workings is different from the workings it witnesses. The meditator knows awareness is distinct from the objects it takes, but this knowledge is not at the verbal level as it is expressed here. Rather, the meditator knows this and each ensuing realization in his direct experience. He may have no words for his realizations; he understands but cannot necessarily state that understanding.

HIGH

DEGREE OF INSIGHT

LOW

NIRODH

TOTAL CESSATION OF CONSCIOUSNESS.

NIRVANA

CONSCIOUSNESS CEASES TO
HAVE AN OBJECT

EFFORTLESS INSIGHT

CONTEMPLATION IS QUICK, EFFORTLESS, INDEFATIGABLE.
INSTANTANEOUS KNOWLEDGE OF ANATTA, ANICCA, DUKKHA.
CESSATION OF PAIN, PERVASIVE EQUANIMITY.

REALIZATION

REALIZATIONS OF THE DREADFUL, UNSATISFACTORY, AND WEARISOME NATURE OF PHYSICAL
AND MENTAL PHENOMENA. PHYSICAL PAIN. ARISING OF DESIRE TO ESCAPE THESE PHENOMENA.
PERCEPTION OF VANISHING OF MIND OBJECTS; PERCEPTION FAST AND
FLAWLESS. DISAPPEARANCE OF LIGHTS, RAPTURE, ETC.

PSEUDONIRVANA

CLEAR PERCEPTION OF THE ARISING AND PASSING OF EACH SUCCESSIVE MIND MOMENT,
ACCOMPANIED BY VARIOUS PHENOMENA SUCH AS BRILLIANT LIGHT, RAPTUROUS
FEELINGS, TRANQUILITY, DEVOTION, ENERGY, HAPPINESS, STRONG MINDFULNESS,
EQUANIMITY TOWARD OBJECTS OF CONTEMPLATION, QUICK AND CLEAR PERCEPTION,
AND ATTACHMENT TO THESE NEWLY ARISEN STATES.

STAGE OF REFLECTIONS

THESE PROCESSES SEEN AS NEITHER PLEASANT NOR RELIABLE. EXPERIENCE OF DUKKHA,
UNSATISFACTORINESS. THESE PROCESSES ARE SEEN TO ARISE AND PASS AWAY AT,
EVERY MOMENT OF CONTEMPLATION. EXPERIENCE OF ANICCA, IMPERMANENCE.
THESE DUAL PROCESSES ARE SEEN AS DEVOID OF SELF. EXPERIENCE OF ANATTA, NOT-SELF.
AWARENESS AND ITS OBJECTS ARE PERCEIVED AT EVERY MOMENT
AS DISTINCT AND SEPARATE PROCESSES.

MINDFULNESS

MINDFULNESS OF BODY FUNCTION, PHYSICAL
SENSATIONS, MENTAL STATES, OR MIND OBJECTS.

ACCESS CONCENTRATION

PREVIOUS ATTAINMENT OF ACCESS
CONCENTRATION ON PATH OF
CONCENTRATION

BARE INSIGHT

ACHIEVEMENT OF ABILITY TO NOTICE ALL PHENOMENA
OF MIND TO POINT WHERE INTERFERING THOUGHTS
DO NOT SERIOUSLY DISTURB PRACTICE.

Fig. 2. Landmarks on the Path of Insight.

Continuing his practice of insight, after the meditator has realized the separate nature of awareness and its objects, he can, with further insight, gain a clear understanding that these dual processes are devoid of self. He sees that they arise as effects of their respective causes, not as the result of direction by any individual agent. Each moment of awareness goes according to its own nature, regardless of "one's will." It becomes certain to the meditator that nowhere in the mind can any abiding entity be detected. This is direct experience of the Buddhist doctrine of *anatta,* literally "not self," that all phenomena have no indwelling personality. This includes even "one's self." The meditator sees his past and future life as merely a conditioned cause-effect process. He no longer doubts whether the "I" really exists; he knows "I am" to be a misconception. He realizes the truth of the words of the Buddha in the Pali Canon:

> Just as when the parts are set together
> There arises the word "chariot,"
> So does the notion of a being
> When the aggregates are present.

Continuing to practice insight, the meditator finds that his witnessing mind and its objects come and go at a frequency beyond his ken. He sees his whole field of awareness in continual flux. The meditator realizes that his world of reality is renewed every mind moment in an endless chain. With this realization, he knows the truth of impermanence (Pali: *anicca*) in the depths of his being.

Finding that these phenomena arise and pass away at every moment, the meditator comes to see them as neither pleasant nor reliable. Disenchantment sets in: What is constantly changing cannot be the basis for any lasting satisfaction. As the meditator realizes his private reality to be devoid of self and ever changing, he is led to a state of detachment from his world of experience. From this detached perspective, the impermanent and impersonal qualities of his mind lead him to see it as a source of suffering (Pali: *dukkha*).

Pseudonirvana: The "Ten Corruptions"

The meditator then continues without any further reflections. After these realizations, the meditator begins to see clearly the beginning and end of each successive moment of awareness. With this clarity of perception, there may occur:

- the vision of a *brilliant light* or luminous form
- *rapturous feelings* that cause goose flesh, tremor in the limbs, the sensation of levitation, and the other attributes of rapture
- *tranquility* in mind and body, making them light, plastic, and wieldy
- *devotional feelings* toward and faith in the meditation teacher, the Buddha, his teachings—including the method of insight itself—and the sangha, accompanied by joyous confidence in the virtues of meditation and the desire to advise friends and relatives to practice it
- *vigor* in meditating, with a steady energy neither too lax nor too tense
- sublime *happiness* suffusing the meditator's body, an unprecedented bliss that seems never-ending and motivates him to tell others of this extraordinary experience
- *quick and clear perception* of each moment of awareness: Noticing is keen, strong, and lucid, and the characteristics of impermanence, nonself, and unsatisfactoriness are clearly understood at once.

- *strong mindfulness* so the meditator effortlessly notices every successive moment of awareness; mindfulness gains a momentum of its own
- *equanimity* toward whatever comes into awareness: No matter what comes into his mind, the meditator maintains a detached neutrality.
- a subtle *attachment* to the lights and other factors listed here and pleasure in their contemplation

The meditator is often elated at the emergence of these ten signs and may speak of them thinking he has attained enlightenment and finished the task of meditation. Even if he does not think they mark his liberation, he may pause to bask in their enjoyment. For this reason, this stage, called "Knowledge of Arising and Passing Away," is subtitled in the Visuddhimagga "The Ten Corruptions of Insight." It is a pseudonirvana. The great danger for the meditator is in "mistaking what is not the Path for the Path" or, in lieu of that, faltering in the further pursuit of insight because of his attachment to these phenomena. Finally, the meditator, either on his own or through advice from his teacher, realizes these experiences to be a landmark along the way rather than his final destination. At this point, he turns the focus of insight on them and on his own attachment to them.

Higher Realizations

As this pseudonirvana gradually diminishes, the meditator's perception of each moment of awareness becomes clearer. He can make increasingly fine discrimination of successive moments until his perception is flawless. As his perception quickens, the ending of each moment of awareness is more clearly perceived than its arising. Finally, the meditator perceives each moment only as it vanishes. He experiences contemplating mind and its object as vanishing in pairs at every moment. The meditator's world of reality is in a constant state of dissolution. A dreadful realization flows from this; the mind becomes gripped with fear. All his thoughts seem fearsome. He sees becoming, that is, thoughts coming into being, as a source of terror. To the meditator everything that enters his awareness—even what might once have been very pleasant—now seems oppressive. He is helpless to avoid this oppression; it is part of every moment.

At this point, the meditator realizes the unsatisfactory quality of all phenomena. The slightest awareness he sees as utterly destitute of any possible satisfaction. In them is nothing but danger. The meditator comes to feel that in all the kinds of becoming there is not a single thing that he can place his hopes in or hold onto. All of his awareness, every thought, every feeling, appears insipid. This includes any state of mind the meditator can conceive. In all the meditator perceives, he sees only suffering and misery.

Feeling this misery in all phenomena, the meditator becomes entirely disgusted with them. Though he continues with the practice of insight, his mind is dominated by feelings of discontent and listlessness toward all its own contents. Even the thought of the happiest sort of life or the most desirable objects seem unattractive and boring. He becomes absolutely dispassionate and adverse toward the multitude of mental stuff—to any kind of becoming, destiny, or state of consciousness.

Effortless Insight

Between the moments of noticing, it occurs to the meditator that only in the ceasing of all mental processes is relief possible. Now his mind no longer fastens onto its contents, and the meditator desires to escape from the suffering due to these phenomena. Painful feelings may flood his body, and he may no longer be able to remain long in one posture. The comfortless nature of mind stuff becomes more evident than ever; the desire for deliverance from it emerges at the root of his being.

With this strong desire for surcease from mental processes, the meditator intensifies his efforts to notice these processes for the very purpose of escaping them. Their nature—their impermanence, the element of suffering, and their voidness of self—become clearly evident. The meditator's body will sometimes undergo severe, sharp pains of growing intensity. His whole body and mind may seem a mass of suffering; restlessness may overwhelm his insight. But by systematically noting these pains, they will cease. At this point, the meditator's ability at simply noticing becomes strong and lucid. At every moment, he knows quite clearly the three characteristics of mental phenomena. One of these three comes to dominate his understanding.

Now the meditator's contemplation proceeds automatically, without special effort, as if borne onward of itself. Feelings of dread, despair, and misery cease. Body pains are absent entirely. The meditator's mind has abandoned both dread and delight. An exceedingly sublime clarity of mind and a pervasive equanimity emerge. The meditator need make no further deliberate effort; noticing continues in a steady flow for hours without his tiring. His meditation has its own momentum, and insight becomes especially quick.

Insight is now on the verge of its culmination; the meditator's noticing of each moment of awareness is keen, strong, and lucid. The meditator instantly knows each moment to be impermanent, painful, or without self as he sees its dissolution. He sees all mental phenomena as limited and circumscribed, devoid of desirability, or alien. His detachment from them is at a peak. His noticing no longer enters into or settles down on any phenomena at all. At this moment, a consciousness arises that takes as its object the "signless, no-occurrence, no-formation": *nirvana.* Awareness of all physical and mental phenomena ceases entirely.

This moment of penetration of nirvana does not, in its first attainment, last even for a second. Immediately following this, the "fruition" moment occurs, when the meditator's mind reflects on the experience of nirvana just past. That experience is a cognitive shock of deepest psychological consequence. Because it is of a realm beyond that of the common-sense reality from which our language is generated, nirvana is a "supramundane reality," describable only in terms of what it is not. Nirvana has no phenomenology, no experiential characteristics. It is the unconditioned state.

Nirvana: Subsequent Changes

The word "nirvana" derives from the negative prefix "nir" and the root "vana," to burn, a metaphorical expression for the extinction of motives for becoming. In nirvana, desire, attachment, and self-interest are burned out. Decisive behavior changes follow from this state of consciousness, and the full realization of nirvana actuates a permanent alteration of the meditator's consciousness per se. With the meditator's realization of nirvana, aspects of his ego and of his normal consciousness are abandoned, never to arise again.

The path of insight differs significantly from the path of concentration on this point: Nirvana *destroys* "defiling" aspects of mental states—hatred, greed, delusion, etc.—whereas jhana merely *suppresses* them. The fruit of nirvana for the meditator is effortless moral purity; in fact, purity becomes his only possible behavior. Jhana smothers the meditator's defilements, but their seeds remain latent in his personality as potentialities. On his emergence from the jhanic state, impure acts again become possible as appropriate trigger situations arise. To attain effortless purity, the meditator's egoism must "die." That is, all of his desires originating from self-interest must cease to control his behavior, which happens through achieving nirvana.

After insight has culminated in the nirvanic state, the meditator's mind remains free of certain motivations and psychological states, which no longer arise. On full maturation of insight, his purity is perfected. By then, he will have utterly given up the potential for impure acts. What was in the early stages effortful for the meditator becomes a self-maintaining state in which attitudes of purity are effortless, choiceless by-products of the state itself.

The number of times the meditator enters the nirvanic state determines his level of mastery, that is, his ability to attain nirvana whenever, wherever, as soon as, and for as long as he wants. But his level of mastery is not the same as nirvana-caused personality changes. He can enter nirvana with a given degree of insight countless times without any subsequent change of his being. The deeper he develops insight prior to entering nirvana, the greater the subsequent changes will be. The nature of nirvana itself is identical at each level of attainment. Since nirvana is the complete extinction of consciousness, it is always the same, though beyond experience. But there are differences between levels of nirvana-caused change. The differences are reckoned in

terms of the meditator's consequent loss of ego and alteration in his normal consciousness after he has emerged from
nirvana. Entering the nirvanic state is his "awakening"; these
subsequent changes are his "deliverance."

The first level of deliverance is that of *Sotapanna,* "stream
enterer." The "stream" entered is that leading to the total
loss of selfish ego, the cessation of all strivings to become.
The meditator becomes a stream enterer at the moment of
reflection after his first penetration of nirvana. He remains
a stream enterer until his insight deepens to the degree
necessary to break through to the next level of attainment.
This final liberation, it is said, is sure to occur "within seven
more lifetimes." The stream enterer loses the following
personality traits: his greed for sensory objects; any resentments strong enough to make him agitated; greed for his
own gain, possessions, or praise; his inability to share with
others; his failure to perceive the relative and illusory nature
of whatever may seem pleasurable or beautiful; his mistaking for permanent what is impermanent *(anicca);* his seeing
a self in what is devoid of self *(anatta);* his adherence to mere
rites, compulsive ritualism, and any belief that this or that
is "the truth"; and his doubts in the utility of the path of
insight meditation. The stream enterer by nature can also no
longer engage in lying, stealing, sexual misconduct, physically harming others, or earning his livelihood at the expense
of others.

When the meditator's insight deepens so that the realizations of dukkha, anatta, or anicca more fully pervade his
awareness, his insight intensifies a quantum level deeper. At
this deeper level both his greed for sense desires and his ill
will weaken further. In addition to what he abandoned with
stream entry, the meditator lets go of gross desires for sense
objects and strong resentment. He is now a *sakadgami,* "once
returner," who will be fully liberated in this lifetime "or the

next." The intensity of his feelings of attraction and aversion diminishes: He can no longer be strongly impelled toward or put off by anything. The pull of sex, for example, lessens; he can still have intercourse for procreation, but he will have no compulsive sexual needs. Impartiality typifies his reactions toward any and all stimuli.

At the next phase in the deepening of his insight, he abandons altogether both greed for sense desires and ill will. What was diminished when he reached the level of once returner is now wholly extinguished. The meditator is an *anagami,* "nonreturner," and he will be totally liberated from the wheel of becoming in his present lifetime. In addition to what he previously abandoned, his last remaining residual propensities toward greed or resentment drop away. All aversion to worldly states, such as loss, disgrace, pain, or blame, ceases. Maliciousness in motivation, volition, or speech becomes impossible for the nonreturner. He can no longer even have a thought of ill will toward anyone, and the category of "enemy" vanishes from his thinking, along with that of "dislike." Similarly, even his subtlest desire for sense objects disappears. Sexual activity, for example, is unlikely for the nonreturner because his feelings of lust are gone, as are his desires for sensual pleasures. Equanimity prevails toward all external objects; their valence to the nonreturner is absolutely neutral.

When the meditator's insight fully matures, he overcomes all remaining fetters to liberation. He is now an *arahant,* an "awakened being" or saint; the word arahant means "one who is worthy" of veneration. The arahant is free from his former socially conditioned identity; he sees consensual concepts of reality as illusions. He is absolutely free from suffering and from acting in a way that would further his karma. Having no feelings of "self," his acts are purely functional, either for maintenance of his body or for the good of others.

The arahant does everything with physical grace. Nothing in his past can cause thoughts of greed, hatred, and the like to come to mind. His past deeds are erased as determinants of behavior, and he is free of his past conditioned habits. He lives fully in the moment; all his actions bespeak spontaneity. The last vestiges of egoism the meditator relinquishes in this final stage include: his desire to seek worldly gain, fame, pleasure, or praise; his desire for even the bliss of the material or formless jhanas; mental stiffness or agitation; covetousness of anything whatsoever. For the arahant, the least tendency toward an unvirtuous thought or deed is literally inconceivable.

With the full extinction of "unwholesome" roots—lust, aggression, and pride—as motives in the meditator's behavior, loving-kindness, altruistic joy, compassion, and equanimity emerge as bases for his actions. Behavior stemming from unwholesome motives is seen as "unskilled"; the arahant's acts are in this sense "skilled." His motives are totally pure. Dreaming, too, changes for the arahant; he has no dreams due to bodily states (e.g., dreams of being chased, being hot or cold) or because of his impressions of daily happenings, but he may have premonitory dreams that foreshadow future events. Though the arahant can experience bodily pain, he bears it with equanimity. A prominent trait of the arahant is unselfishness, likened in the Pali Canon to motherly love:

> Even as a mother watches over her only begotten child, so let his heart and mind be filled with boundless love for all creatures, great and small, let him practice benevolence towards the whole world, above, below, across, without exception, and let him set himself utterly free from ill-will and enmity.

One who has "awakened" in this way is capable of a dual perception: "Knowing how everything actually is, and how everything appears." For the arahant, normal reality is perceived simultaneously with the validity of the "noble truths" of impermanence, suffering and nonselfhood. Both these perceptual levels are evident at every moment. For example, even worldly pleasures are a form of suffering. Wei Wu Wei (1968: p. 61) says of the meaning of suffering at the arahant's level of consciousness:

When the Buddha found that he was Awake . . . it may be assumed that he observed that what hitherto he had regarded as happiness, as compared to suffering, was such no longer. His only standard henceforward was *ananda* or what we try to think of as bliss. Suffering he saw as the negative form of happiness, happiness as the positive form of suffering, respectively the negative and positive aspects of experience. But relative to the noumenal state which now alone he knew, both could be described . . . as *dukkha* (suffering). *Dukkha* was the counterpart of *sukha* which implied "ease and well-being," . . . to the Buddha nothing phenomenal could appear to be *sukha* although in phenomenality it might so appear in contrast to *dukkha*.

The way the arahant might understand the truth of nonself is more straightforward. As D. T. Suzuki (1958: p. 293) puts it, the arahant finds "by immediate knowledge that when one's heart was cleansed of the defilements of the ordinary ego-centered impulses and desires, nothing was left there to claim itself as ego-residuum." More simply, after the meditator has let go of his selfish ego to become an arahant, he finds he has no "self" left.

For the arahant, perception in insight meditation is perfected: He witnesses the most minute segments of his mind's
working, the chain of mind moments. According to this
tradition, the Buddha witnessed 17×10^{21} mind moments
in "the wink of an eye," each one distinct and different from
the one preceding and the one following it. Like him, the
arahant sees that the smallest pieces of the mosaic of consciousness are changing at every moment. Nothing in the
universe of his mind is constant. Since his external reality
flows from his internal universe, nowhere can he find any
stability or permanence.

Total Cessation

There is a state similar to nirvana (little known in the West)
called *nirodh* (cessation). In nirvana, there is the cessation of
consciousness; in nirodh, bodily processes become quiescent.
This absolute cessation of consciousness is extremely difficult
to attain. Nirodh is accessible only to a nonreturner or an
arahant, and only if he has also mastered all eight jhanas.
Neither a stream enterer nor a once returner has given up
enough ego-bound attachments to muster the superconcen-
tration required for nirodh. In gaining access to this state of
total nonoccurrence, even the slightest sense desire is an
obstacle.

On the path to nirodh, the meditator practices insight,
using as a base each jhana in succession up to the eighth,
"neither perception nor nonperception." With the cessation
of this last state of ultrasubtle consciousness, he enters nirodh. The cessation of nirodh is said to be "differently real,"
for all the data of our experience of reality, even the most
subtle states, are absent.

Although nirodh can last for up to seven days of the

human time rhythm, there is no time sequence in the state itself: The moment immediately preceding and that immediately following it seem in succession. The limit of seven days given for nirodh may be due to its unique physiology. The meditator's heartbeat and normal metabolism, it is said, cease along with consciousness (or, more likely, continue below the threshold of perception). Metabolic processes continue at a residual level, and the meditator's body does not decay like a corpse. The meditator must set a predetermined length of time for his stay in this state before he enters. On emerging from it, he goes through the jhanas in reverse order to normal consciousness. At the eighth jhana, awareness resumes; at the third, normal bodily function; at the first, thoughts and sense perception.

At their highest extremes, the path of concentration through the jhanas and the path of insight to nirvana tend to meet. Even so, there remain extremely subtle but crucial differences between these rarefied states of consciousness. In the seventh jhana, "no-thing-ness," awareness is of objectless consciousness. In the eighth jhana, even no-thing-ness is not present; yet it remains as a latent function, and so no-thing-ness cannot be said *not* to exist: this is the supersubtle realm of "neither perception nor nonperception." In nirvana, consciousness is on the brink of extinction with the awareness of no consciousness at all. The cessation of awareness culminates in nirodh, in which there is no awareness whatsoever. Attaining even the highest jhanas does not lastingly alter the meditator's personality, while nirvana does so irrevocably.

These different paths mark two extremes in exploring and controlling the mind. A meditator who could marshal enough one-pointedness to attain the formless jhanas might easily enter the nirvanic state should he choose to turn his powerful concentration to watching his own mind. Conversely, a meditator who had entered the nirvanic state might well be so indifferent to hindrances and distractions that, should he choose to focus on a single object of awareness, he would readily enter and proceed through the jhanic levels. Those who traverse these distinctly different paths to their summits, then, may no longer belong solely to one but to both. With full mastery of either concentration or insight, the other is readily attainable. At their end, the distinction between meditation avenues melts.

PART TWO

MEDITATION PATHS: A SURVEY

Experience is the forerunner of all spiritual teachings, but the same experience can be expressed differently. In any given tradition, the map of meditative states set down is to some degree arbitrary. The map is not the territory, and the terrain traversed in meditation is nebulous to begin with. It is little wonder that maps of meditative states seem so different from one another. Lao Tzu recognizes this dilemma in the *Tao Te Ching:*

> The way that can be told
> Is not the constant way;
> The name that can be named
> Is not the constant name.

The Tibetans recognize two levels of religion: "the expedient teaching" and "the final teaching." The expedient teachings are the multitude of world religions, each shaped by and for the people who adhere to it. Part of the differences between meditation maps stem from this level. The survey of meditation maps in this chapter is aimed at the level of final teaching, in which doctrinal differences fall away. Here the unity of practice comes into focus. Religions may differ by virtue of accident of time and place, but the experiences that are precursors to beliefs are often the same. Some degree of unity in final teaching is inevitable: All human beings are alike in nervous system, and it is at this level that the laws governing final teaching operate.

The Visuddhimagga map undercuts seeming distinctions between spiritual paths in meditation techniques and states. These distinctions, in fact, stem from different ideologies. The Visuddhimagga road maps give us a typology for sorting out techniques in terms of their mechanics, cutting through the conceptual overlay of religions. This survey is meant to be seminal, not exhaustive. In most cases, I discuss only one illustrative technique of the many disciplines belonging to a given spiritual path. This comparison is one of parts, of specific practices and states, rather than a taxonomy of spiritual paths.

I based most of the summaries that follow on published sources rather than on my personal investigation. They may, therefore, seem incomplete or imprecise to a person on any of these paths. Each path is a living tradition that presents itself differently to each person according to his needs and circumstances.

The summaries are didactic, not definitive. My intent is to give those not involved in them an idea of what they are like. I discuss each path in enough detail to show its unique flavor, while demonstrating its points of similarity with other paths.

4. HINDU BHAKTI

Sri Ramakrishna, a Bengali saint at the turn of the century, once went to a theater performance of the life of Sri Chaitanya, the seventeenth-century Bhakti saint known for his songs and dances of love for Lord Krishna. At several points during the play, on seeing portrayals of Chaitanya's devotion to Krishna, Ramakrishna entered samadhi, a deep meditative absorption.

Ramakrishna's samadhi marks him as a Bhakta par excellence. Bhakti, or devotion to a divine being, is the most popular form of worship in contemporary world religions. A Christian singing "Amazing Grace," a Hassidic Jew dancing and singing at the Wailing Wall, a Sufi reciting "El Allah Hu," a Hindu chanting "Hare Krishna," and a Japanese Buddhist repeating "Na-mu-a-mi-da-bu-tsu, Na-mu-a-mi-da-bu-tsu" are all engaged in more or less the same devotional process, though directed toward different divine beings.

Bhakti is the strongest school of religious practice in Hinduism; its roots are ancient. In the classic *Srimad Bhagavatam,* remembering or constant chanting of Krishna's name is recommended over all other practices as the best path for this age. The *Kalisantaram Upanishad* has Brahma extol to the bard Narada as the highest or *maha-*mantra, "Hare Rama, Hare Krishna"—Hare, Rama, and Krishna all being manifestations of Vishnu. The essence of Bhakti is making the object of devotion one's central thought. The devotee may choose any deity or divine being as his devotional object, or *ishta.* The thrust of his practice is to keep the thought of the ishta foremost in his mind at all times. Besides *kirtan* (chanting or singing), there are three levels of *japa,* repetition of the name: spoken, silent verbalization, and mental. Some regard each succeeding form of japa as "ten times" more efficacious than the preceding one (Poddar, 1965).

Poddar suggests that the neophyte practice a minimum of six hours of japa per day. From the beginning, the devotee also strives to maintain japa in the midst of life's activities. The *mala,* or rosary, is a common technical aid to japa; with the telling of each bead, the devotee recites the name once. Other aids include gearing recitation to each breath or to every beat of the pulse. No matter what the mnemonic device, the principle is the same: The devotee returns his attention to the ishta at once whenever his mind ceases to be engaged elsewhere. The goal of this stage of practice is to make the habit of repetition stronger than all the devotee's other mental habits. Gradually, his mind will be occupied solely with the thought of the deity or centered on it as other thoughts come and go on the periphery of awareness. In this way, the devotee becomes one-pointed on his ishta.

Some advice to the devotee repeats the Visuddhimagga. Because the mental habit of constant worship through remembering is at first vulnerable to other pulls for attention, the devotee is urged to keep to *satsang,* the company of persons on the same path. Staying with satsang counters the pull of worldly attachments, as does *darshan,* the visiting of saints. The devotee is further urged to avoid talk of "women, wealth, unbelievers, and enemies." The devotee's success depends on virtue: Purity, says Vivekananda (1964), "is absolutely the basic work, the bedrock upon which the whole Bhakti-building rests." In giving advice to her own disciples, Ananda Mayee Ma, the late Indian woman saint, echoes the Visuddhimagga for Buddhist monks (1972: pp. 126–129):

Indolence and lust—these two are the greatest obstacles on the path . . . Choose carefully and abide strictly by such occupations as awaken godly thoughts and feelings . . . Engage in them even when there is no desire so to do, as one takes medicine . . . Food, sleep, toilet, clothes, etc., should be given only as much attention as is needed for the maintenance of health . . . Anger, greed and the like must be altogether abandoned. Neither should you be swayed by praise or prestige.

The guru's help ranks in importance with purity for the devotee's progress. Ananda Mayee Ma (1972) compared the role of the guru to that of experts in any specialized field to whom one must turn in order to become proficient. But the function of the guru transcends that of the worldly expert. In addition to directing the disciple, the guru is also the intermediary for divine grace needed for the disciple's efforts to bear fruit. No matter how diligent the devotee, without the guru's blessings his efforts are useless.

Ramana Maharshi (1962) says of "Guru-kripa," surrender to a master whose grace descends on the devotee, "If one's surrender is complete, all sense of self is lost." When the devotee surrenders to the pure being of the guru, his mind becomes purified. The purified mind easily stills, allowing the devotee to turn inward in meditation and find the self. This is the guru's "grace," which is in fact immanent in the devotee. There is, says Ramana Maharshi, no difference between God, guru, and self: The external guru helps the devotee find the internal self in meditation. The outer guide leads the devotee back within himself.

As in all paths, virtue—in the beginning an act of will—becomes a by-product of the practice itself. As the devotee's mind focuses on his devotional object, it withdraws from worldly objects. By love of God, says Vivekananda, love of the pleasures of the senses and of the intellect is all made dim. As his consciousness becomes more thoroughly imbued with the thought of his ishta, the devotee finds worldly delights repugnant. By this point, observes Poddar (1965), "compared to the joy of repeating the 'Rama nama' (i.e., mantra) all other enjoyments of the world are insipid."

Bhakti begins in duality, with the devotee separate from his ishta, as from any love object. The *Bhakti Sutras,* in fact, have a typology of Divine Love that includes loving the ishta as one's friend, as one's spouse, and as one's child. Prabhavananda and Isherwood (1969) suggest that "all human relationships may be sublimated through the practice of Bhakti yoga." Though this love may begin with the forms of, and energies invested in, interpersonal love, it ends in union with the state of love evoked by the love object. Here, says Vivekananda, "Love, the Lover, and the Beloved are One." With this union, Bhakti merges into the path of jhana. The fruit of japa is constant remembrance at every waking moment of the beloved. This yields a "love intoxication"; its signs are ecstasy and absorption. The feelings of bliss, rapture, and joy of this intoxication characterize access concentration. The love-intoxicated devotee's behavior, however, is sometimes as erratic as a madman's. The *Srimad Bhagavatam* (XI, ii) describes this stage:

> The devotee loses all sense of decorum and moves about in the world unattached . . . His heart melts through love as he habitually chants the Name of his beloved lord, and like one possessed, he now bursts into peals of laughter, now weeps, now cries, now sings aloud and now begins to dance.

The enraptured devotee is on the threshold of samadhi, or jhana. His ecstasy indicates the access level; he verges on the first jhana. Should he concentrate with enough intensity on his ishta, he can enter samadhi. Once samadhi is reached, according to Swami Muktananda (1971), there is no further need for chanting or japa: They are a prelude to the deep meditation of samadhi. An accomplished bhakta can attain samadhi on the least stimulus suggesting his devotion, as did Sri Ramakrishna.

The initial power of Bhakti is the element of interpersonal love felt by the devotee toward his deity. As he progresses on this path, that love changes from an interpersonal to a transcendental or transpersonal love. The devotee no longer depends on the object of devotion to bestow bliss. Rather, he finds that the transcendental states of which the bliss is one aspect exist within himself. He need no longer cling to the external form of his devotional object; the states once evoked by his beloved's form have come to be fixtures of his own consciousness. Sankaracharya, the founder of Advait Hinduism, noted that Bhakti ends in a quest for the self—a major difference between Buddhism, which seeks to dissolve the sense of self, and Hindu paths, which aim at uniting the seeker with a "higher" self. In Bhakti, what begins as an external evocation of love becomes in the end an internal absorption in which the devotee in samadhi delights uninterruptedly in "pure *self.*"

The devotee brings his mind to one-pointedness through constant remembrance of the ishta and so finally reaches samadhi at the level of first jhana. But if he is to go beyond this level, he must transcend his own devotional object. Any thought of name and form, even that of a deity, binds the devotee to the first jhana. Sri Ramakrishna, for example, for many years an ardent devotee of the Divine Mother, had experienced many visions and states of bliss as Her devotee. Later, he took initiation from a naked ascetic (Swami Saradananda, 1963: p. 255):

After initiating me . . . the Naked One asked me to make my mind free of function in all respects, and merge in the meditation of the Self. But, when I sat for meditation, I could by no means make my mind go beyond the bounds of name and form and cease functioning. The mind withdrew itself from all other things, but as soon as it did so, the intimately familiar form of the universal Mother appeared . . . But, at last, collecting all the strength of my will, I cut Mother's form to pieces with the sword of discrimination . . . There remained no function in the mind, which transcended quickly the realm of names and forms, making me merge in samadhi.

The Visuddhimagga says that on initial entry to a new plane of meditative consciousness the meditator must cut his ties to the preceding plane. Each plane has its special points of appeal, some exceedingly sublime. The prerequisite for gaining the next higher level is to become detached from the lower plane, as Ramakrishna did, lest awareness be pulled back to it. For the devotee, this means that his ishta's form must finally be abandoned in favor of becoming himself, in samadhi, that manifestation of pure being for which the ishta is himself worshiped.

Beyond the attainment of samadhi, there is a state in which a samadhilike awareness diffuses throughout all the devotee's activities. Japa, if developed to this point, repeats as if of itself virtually every moment, day and night. This state is sahaj samadhi and marks the end point in the devotee's spiritual evolution. In sahaj samadhi, there is no distinction between the devotee, the world, and the ishta; his perception of self and the world shifts radically. As Vivekananda (1964: p. 90) puts it, "When a person loves the Lord, the whole universe becomes dear to him . . . his whole nature is purified and completely changed." Renunciation becomes effortless, all attachments save to the beloved ishta having fallen away.

From this intense and all-absorbing love comes faith and self-surrender, the conviction that nothing that happens is against one: "Not my, but Thy will be done." This selflessness is evident in the words of Ananda Mayee Ma, speaking of herself (1972: p. 37): "Truly this body belongs to all; for this reason it behaves and speaks, as far as possible, so as to fulfill the needs of the people with whom it deals at any particular time." One at this ultimate point on the Bhakti path perceives the sacred within the secular; everything is sacred because it bespeaks the beloved. The devotee need no longer observe any special forms or symbols for worship. He worships in his heart, the world having become his altar. Kabir (1970: pp. 48–49) eloquently sums up his own experience of this state:

O Sadhu! the simple union is the best,
Since the day when I met with my Lord, there has been
   no end to the sport of our love.
I shut not my eyes, I close not my ears, I do not
   mortify my body;
I see with eyes open and smile, and behold His beauty
   everywhere;
I utter His Name, and whatever I see, it reminds me of
   Him; whatever I do, it becomes His worship.
The rising and setting are one to me; all contradictions
   are solved.
Wherever I go, I move round Him,
All I achieve is His service:
When I lie down, I lie prostrate at His feet.

He is the only adorable one to me: I have none other.
My tongue has left off impure words, it sings His glory
    day and night:
Whether I rise or sit down, I can never forget Him; for
    the rhythm of His music beats in my ears.
Kabir says, I am immersed in the one great bliss which
    transcends all pleasure and pain.

5. JEWISH MEDITATION

"In every religion," writes the contemporary Kabbalist Z'ev
ben Shimon Halevi (1976), "there are always two aspects,
the seen and the hidden." The seen manifests as rituals,
scriptures, services; the hidden bears the light that should
illumine these forms. In Judaism, the hidden teachings are
called Kabbalah. These teachings, it is said, originated with
the angels, who were instructed by God. Kabbalists identify
the great figures of biblical times—Abraham, David, the
Prophets—as well as the Essenes and other mystical groups
of Jewish history, as bearers of this tradition. Halevi says
Joshua ben Miriam, otherwise known as Jesus, was a transmitter of Kabbalah. This hidden Jewish tradition first sur-
faced in Europe in the Middle Ages, and many lineages of
its transmission continue to the present day.

The cosmology of Kabbalah posits a multileveled reality,
each level a complete world in itself. These planes are arranged hierarchically, the upper part of each corresponding
to the lower aspect of the one above. The highest sphere is
that of Metatron, the chief archangel, who teaches human
beings. Each level embodies a state of consciousness, and
most people exist at the lowest levels—mineral, vegetable,

animal. In the Kabbalist view, normal man is incomplete, restricted as he is to these lower planes. He lives a mechanical life, bound by the rhythms of his body and by habitual reactions and perceptions; he blindly seeks pleasure and avoids pain. While he may have brief glimpses of higher possibilities, he has no desire to raise his level of awareness. Kabbalah seeks to awaken the student to his own limitations and to train him to enter a state of consciousness in which he becomes in tune with a higher awareness, no longer a slave of his body and conditioning. To become free, the aspirant must first become disillusioned with the mechanical games of life. He then builds a foundation for entry into a higher consciousness, the Paradise within. This, says Halevi, is the allegorical meaning of the bondage in Egypt: the slavery of the limited ego, the seeker's purification in the desert, and his entry into the land of milk and honey.

To achieve his task, the Kabbalist must observe the working of the *Yesod,* his ordinary mind or ego, so as to see through his own foibles and self-delusions and bring into awareness the unconscious forces that shape his thoughts and actions. To do this, he seeks to reach the level of awareness called *Tiferet,* a state of clarity that is witness or "watcher" of the Yesod. From this state of heightened self-awareness emanates what is sometimes seen as a guardian angel that guides one through difficult situations with ease and skill. Tiferet is beyond the ordinary mind dealing with everyday matters; here ego is transcended. It is the realm of the spirit, the bridge between man and the divine, the gate of Paradise. It is the soul. Thus, in a state of Yesod, the ego rules; when Tiferet is dominant, a higher state occurs in which one looks down on oneself. This state of awakened consciousness is typically glimpsed only briefly in the ordinary man's life. The Kabbalist seeks to gain permanent entry to this state and ascend to even higher levels still.

The specifics of the Kabbalist's training—his foundation for higher states—vary from school to school, though the basics are fairly constant. When the aspirant contacts a *Maggid,* or teacher, his training begins in earnest. The Maggid directs him in candid self-observation, using the stuff of the student's life as material for teaching. There are many systems that aid the seeker in knowing himself, such as an intricate numerology that transmutes Hebrew letters and words into a number code with mystical interpretations. One of the best-known Kabbalist systems is the Tree of Life, a map of the hierarchies and attributes of the many planes that interplay in the world and within man. The tree serves as a template through which the aspirant observes his own nature and a key to unlock the hidden dimensions guiding his life. But a mere intellectual understanding of the tree may be Yesodic, in the service of the ego. No matter how elegantly the seeker grasps the intricacies of the tree, his studies will be for naught if he neglects his spiritual development. The prerequisite is training of his will, his capacity for unwavering attention. For this the Kabbalist turns to meditation. Writes Halevi (1976: p. 126):

> Preparation means to be able to receive and impart
> . . . the degree of reception determines the quality of
> Knowledge given. The exchange is precise, and is paid
> for by the amount of conscious attention in a complex
> situation. Where attention is, there is power.

The instructions for meditation form part of the secret teachings of Kabbalists and, apart from general rules, are not made public. Each student learns from the mouth of his Maggid. In general, meditation in Kabbalah is an offshoot of the normal prayers of the devout Jew. Meditative concentration allows the Kabbalist to delve to the depths of a particular subject—a word in a prayer or an aspect of the tree—and also to arrest his thought so as to remain one-pointed on the subject. This fine focus is *kavvanah,* cleaving of thought to a single subject. In one sort of kavvanah, the meditator concentrates on each word of regular prayer with his full attention, to the point at which his mind transcends the simple meaning of the words, and so uses them as a vehicle to a higher state. Azriel of Gerona, a medieval Kabbalist, described the process of kavvanah as when "thought expands and ascends to its origin, so that when it reaches it, it ends and cannot ascend any further." As a result of this state, the words of the prayer become transmuted, full of a divine influx from this nothingness of thought.

According to Kabbalist lore, the entry into the inner Paradise by one who has not properly prepared a foundation through self-purification can be dangerous. The Talmud tells the story of four rabbis who entered Paradise: one went mad, one died, and another lost faith; only one, Rabbi Akiba, came back in peace. The influential writings of Abraham Abulafia, among the most detailed elaboration of Kabbalist meditation, were designed to teach a safe approach to the inner Paradise. Abulafia's meditation combines various letters of the Hebrew alphabet in a meditation on the holy names of God. This method is distinct from prayer; the aspirant devoted himself to it in seclusion rather than in synagogue, at given hours and under guidance of his Maggid. Halevi describes the path traveled by one who practices such a meditation. As he repeats the name, he directs his attention upward from Yesod, the limited ordinary mind, into Tiferet, an awareness beyond ego. That is, he directs his thought away from all forms of this world, focusing on the name. If his efforts meet with God's grace, the self will suddenly rise up beyond Tiferet to an ecstatic state called *Daat,* or knowledge. Here his sense of separation from God dissolves, if only for a moment. He is filled with a great joy, and seized by a sweet rapture. When he emerges from this state, he will again become aware of the inner repetition of the name, which he had transcended for that instant in a state the Theravadans might call jhana.

The end of the Kabbalist's path is *devekut,* in which the seeker's soul cleaves to God. When the Kabbalist stabilizes his consciousness at this level, he is no longer an ordinary man but a supernatural man, a *Zaddik,* or saint, who has escaped the chains of his personal ego. The qualities of one who has attained this station include equanimity, indifference to praise or blame, a sense of being alone with God, and prophecy. The ego's will is submerged in the divine will so that one's acts serve God rather than a limited self. He need no longer study Torah, for he has *become* Torah. One classical commentator defines devekut as a state of mind in which (Scholem, 1974: p. 175):

> You constantly remember God and his love, nor do you remove your thought from Him . . . to the point when such a person speaks with someone else, his heart is not with them at all but is still before God. And indeed it may be true of those who attain this rank, that their soul is granted immortal life even in this lifetime, for they are themselves a dwelling place for the Holy Spirit.

6. CHRISTIAN MEDITATION

The first Christian monks were hermits who lived during the fourth century A.D. in the most remote parts of the barren Egyptian desert. A record from that time (Waddell, 1957: p. 57) has it that "once a certain brother brought a bunch of grapes to the holy Macarius," one of the hermits. But the hermit

> who for love's sake thought not on his own things but on the things of others, carried it to another brother, who seemed more feeble. And the sick man gave thanks to God for the kindness of his brother, but he too thinking more of his neighbor than himself, brought it to another, and he again to another, and so that same bunch of grapes was carried round all the cells scattered as they were far over the desert, and no one knowing who first had sent it, it was brought at last to the first giver.

The Desert Fathers, like present-day Indian yogis in the high Himalayas, sought out the isolation of the harshest desert to commune with God free of worldly distractions. The meditation practices and rules for living of these earliest Christian monks bear strong similarity to those of their Hindu and Buddhist renunciate brethren several kingdoms to the east. While Jesus and his teachings were their inspiration, the meditative techniques they adopted for finding their God suggest either a borrowing from the East or a spontaneous rediscovery. The ways of the Desert Fathers influence Christian monasticism to this day; their selfless love remains a guiding example.

Constant remembrance of God—much as the Bhakti and the Kabbalist aim for—has been a mainstay of Christian worship from the beginning, though the present-day use of rosary beads is a dim remainder of more wholehearted remembrance. Thomas Merton (1960) observes that what is today practiced as "prayer" in Christian churches is but one—albeit the surviving one—of a range of more intensive contemplative practices. The Desert Fathers meditated with verbal or silent repetition of a single phrase from the Scriptures, a Christian equivalent of mantra. The most popular was the prayer of the Publican: "Lord Jesus Christ, Son of God, have mercy on me a sinner." In its short form, *Kyrie eleison,* it was repeated silently throughout the day "until it became as spontaneous and instinctive as breathing."

The Desert Fathers emphasized purity, and their ascetic acts are fabled; St. Simeon the Stylite, who lived thirty years atop a pillar, was one of the best known. As in the Visuddhimagga, purification was used to aid concentration; in the words of one of the fathers, "the soul, unless it be cleansed of alien thoughts, cannot pray to God in contemplation." A corollary maxim is that life in the world matters only insofar as it reflects an inner life of contemplative practice. The spirit of this tradition, preserved in modern monastic orders such as the Benedictine Trappists, is summed up by St. Abba Dorotheus, an early Desert Father, in giving directions on spiritual training (Kadloubovsky and Palmer, 1969: p. 161):

> Over whatever you have to do, even if it be very urgent and demands great care, I would not have you argue or be agitated. For rest assured, everything you do, be it great or small, is but one-eighth of the problem, whereas to keep one's state undisturbed even if thereby one should fail to accomplish the task, is the other seven-eighths. So if you are busy at some task and wish to do it perfectly, try to accomplish it—which, as I said would be one-eighth of the problem, and at the same time to preserve your state unharmed—which constitutes seven-eighths. If, however, in order to accomplish your task you would inevitably be carried

away and harm yourself or another by arguing with him, you should not lose seven for the sake of preserving one-eighth.

One major tradition stemming from the practices of the Desert Fathers, though virtually lost in Western Christendom, has changed little in Eastern Orthodoxy since the first millenium of Christianity. This is the practice of the Prayer of Jesus. Its repetition fulfills Paul's injunction to "pray always." The early fathers called it "the art of arts and the science of sciences," which leads the seeker toward the highest human perfection. This tradition is preserved in the collection of early Christian writings known as the *Philokalia* (Kadloubovsky and Palmer, 1971). Its translation from Greek to Russian at the turn of the century came on the crest of a wave of revival of the practice throughout Russia (French, 1970).

The practice of the Prayer develops strength of concentration. As in Hindu Bhakti, the prerequisites for success with the Prayer are "genuine humility, sincerity, endurance, purity." Hesychius of Jerusalem, a fifth-century teacher of the uses of the Jesus Prayer (known now in the West as Hesychasm), describes it as a spiritual art that releases one completely from passionate thoughts, words, and evil deeds, and gives a "sure knowledge of God the Incomprehensible." Practice of the Prayer brings purity of heart, which is the "same as guarding the mind, kept perfectly free of all fantasies" and all thoughts. The way to this purity is unceasingly calling upon Christ, with perfect attention, resisting all other thoughts. Hesychius describes thoughts as "enemies who are bodiless and invisible, malicious and clever at harming us, skillful, nimble and practised in warfare," who enter in through the five senses. A mind caught in the senses or

in thought is distant from Jesus. To overcome sense consciousness and attain a silent mind is to be with Him.

Among the "Directions to Hesychasts" is the instruction
to find a teacher who bears the spirit within him. Once
found, the seeker devotes himself to his master, obeying all
his commands. Other directions include seclusion in a quiet,
dimly lit cell, eating only as much as one needs to keep alive,
silence, full performance of church ritual, fasting, vigils, and
most important, practice of the Prayer.

The *Philokalia* quotes St. Nilus: "He who wishes to see
what his mind really is must free himself of all thoughts;
then he will see it like a sapphire or the hue of heaven." His
instructions for stilling the mind specify sitting on a low
stool in the solitude of one's cell on first awakening and for
an hour (or more, if one is able), "collect your mind from
its customary circling and wandering outside, and quietly
lead it into the heart by way of breathing, keeping this
prayer: 'Lord Jesus Christ, Son of God, have mercy on me!'
connected with the breath." When with practice it becomes
possible to so pray with perfect one-pointedness, "then,
abandoning the many and the varied, we shall unite with the
One, the Single and the Unifying, directly in a union which
transcends reason"—presumably, in jhana.

Prayer is not to be limited to specific sessions but practiced
without distraction in the midst of every activity. The
Prayer so performed brings purity to worldly activity. The
monk who has mastered this ability has the stature of Christ
because he enjoys perfect purity of heart. The goal of the
Desert Fathers' efforts was what Merton calls a "nowhere-
ness and no-mindness"—a condition known by the name
quies, literally "rest"—the monk having lost all preoccupation with his limited self. Combined with ascetic life in the
desert, these prayer practices, in the words of Merton, "ena-
bled the old superficial self to be purged away and permitted

the gradual emergence of the true, secret self in which the
Believer and Christ were 'one spirit.' " St. Isaac comments
that one who has attained a state of effortless, constant prayer
(Kadloubovsky and Palmer, 1971: p. 213)

> has reached the summit of all virtues, and has become
> the abode of the Holy Spirit. . . . when the Holy Spirit
> comes to live in a man, he never ceases to pray, for then
> the Holy Spirit constantly prays in him. . . . In eating
> or drinking, sleeping or doing something, even in deep
> sleep his heart sends forth without effort the incense and
> sighs of prayer.

The themes of acts of purification, deep meditation, and
finally their fruition in spontaneous purity and constant
remembrance of God are not unique to Eastern Orthodoxy's
Hesychasts. These central threads are widespread in Catholic
contemplative traditions. St. Augustine, for one, advocated
these same basic practices. Furthermore, the similarity of
entry into jhana and the union with the One of the Christian
mystic is clear in St. Augustine's *Confessions*. Augustine
advocated a long process of self-denial, self-conquest, and
the practice of virtue as preparation for "the ascent to the
contemplation of God." Only such ascetic self-discipline can
bring about the readjustment of character prerequisite for
entry into the higher stages of a spiritual life. Augustine is
insistent that not until the monk has so become "cleansed
and healed" can he begin the proper practice of what he calls
"contemplation." Contemplation itself entails "recollection" and "introversion." Recollection is concentrating the
mind, banishing all images, thoughts, and sense perceptions.
Having emptied the mind of all distractions, introversion
can begin. Introversion concentrates the mind on its own
deepest part in what is seen as the final step before the soul

finds God: "The mind abstracts itself from all the bodily senses, as interrupting and confounding it with their din, in order to see itself in itself." So seeing, the soul arrives at God "in and above itself." Augustine describes the physical side of the state induced by this experience in terms like the Visuddhimagga's fourth jhana (Butler, 1966: p. 50):

> When the attention of the mind is wholly turned away and withdrawn from the bodily senses, it is called an ecstasy. Then whatever bodies may be present are not seen with the open eyes, nor any voices heard at all. It is a state midway between sleep and death: The soul is rapt in such wise as to be withdrawn from the bodily senses more than in sleep, but less than in death.

St. Benedict's still definitive *Rule for Monasteries* depicts this progression in terms of degrees of "humility" or purity. At the twelfth and highest degree, the monk not only seems by all appearances to be humble but also has a genuine internal humility. His humility stems from a constant thought very much like the Prayer of the Publican: "Lord I am a sinner and not worthy to lift up my eyes to heaven." At this point, formerly effortful self-discipline becomes effortless (Doyle, 1948: pp. 28–29):

> Having climbed all these steps of humility, therefore, the monk will presently come to that perfect love of God which casts out fear. And all those precepts which formerly he had not observed without fear, he will now begin to keep by reason of that love, without any effort, as though naturally and by habit. No longer will his motive be the fear of hell, but rather the love of Christ, good habit and delight in the virtues which the Lord will deign to show forth by the Holy Spirit in His servant now cleaned from vice and sin.

7. SUFISM

For the Sufi, the basic human weakness is being bound by the lower self. The saints have overcome their lower nature, and novices seek to escape it. Meditation is essential in the novice's efforts to purify his heart. "Meditation for one hour," said an early Sufi master, "is better than ritual worship for a whole year."

The main meditation among Sufis is *zikr,* which means "remembrance." The zikr par excellence is *La ilāha illā 'llah:* "There is no god but God." Bishi al-Hafi, an early Sufi of Baghdad, said, "The Sufi is he who keeps his Heart pure." The Sufi aims for a purity that is total and permanent. The way to this purity is constant remembrance of God. The Prophet Muhammed himself said, "There is a polish for everything that taketh away rust; and the polish of the Heart is the invocation of Allah." Remembrance of God through repeating his name purifies the seeker's mind and opens his heart to Him. A zikr, for example, always accompanies Sufi dancing; it enhances the dance's effect to maintain the remembrance of God throughout. "The dance opens a door in the soul to divine influences," wrote Sultan Walad, Rumi's son. "The dance is good when it arises from remembrance of the Beloved."

Zikr is also a solitary meditation. At first, it is an oral repetition, later a silent one; a fourteenth-century manuscript says, "When the heart begins to recite, the tongue should stop." The goal of zikr, as in all meditation systems, is to overcome the mind's natural state of carelessness and inattention. His mind mastered, the Sufi can become one-pointed on God. The Sufi comment on normal consciousness is that humans are "asleep in a nightmare of unfulfilled

desires," that with the transcendence mental discipline
brings, these desires fall away.

The normal state of attention—scattered and random,
thoughtless and heedless—is the mode of the profane. Remembrance, which anchors the Sufi's mind on God, focuses
his attention and allows him to turn away from the pulls of
the world. A ninth-century Egyptian Sufi commented on
the special efforts the seeker makes: "The repentance of the
masses is from sins, whereas repentance of the elect is from
distraction." After intensive practice of meditation or group
chanting, the following relaxation of efforts may bring a
floodtide of old habits of mind. The degree of such a relapse
serves as a gauge of spiritual progress. No virtue is acquired
if the conditioned habits and reactions take control as soon
as the seeker's intensity lessens.

There is an interplay between effort and grace on the Sufi
path. An eleventh-century itinerary of the Sufi path by
al-Qushari lists the spiritual stations *(maqam)* due to one's
own efforts. These purificatory acts prepare the Sufi for
achieving states *(hal)* that are independent of his own effort.
These effortless states are the gift of God. The first station
is that of "conversion," in which the Sufi resolves to abandon worldly life and devote himself to spiritual seeking.
Then come a number of efforts at self-purification. These
include outright struggle against his own carnal nature,
helped by withdrawal into solitude for ridding himself of
evil habits. At this stage, the Sufi may minimize his involvement in worldly activities and renounce even wholesome
pleasures ordinarily permitted him. He may become a voluntary pauper, accepting his tribulations as tests of purity
and practicing contentment with whatever comes his way.
This last station merges into the first God-given state, satisfaction with things as they are ordained by God.

The central premise supporting these renunciatory acts

permeates Sufi thought: Abu Said of Mineh framed it as follows (Rice, 1964: p. 34): "When occupied with self, you are separated from God. The way to God is but one step; the step out of yourself." Al-Ghazali, a twelfth-century legalist turned Sufi, commented on the essence of the way of the Sufi (Nicholson, 1929: p. 39):

> The gift of the doctrine lies in overcoming the appetites of the flesh and getting rid of its evil dispositions and vile qualities, so that the heart may be cleared of all but God; and the means of clearing it is dhikr Allah, commemoration of God and the concentration of every thought upon Him.

Along his way to desirelessness, the Sufi undergoes states typical of progress in many other kinds of meditation. *Qurb* is a sense of God's constant nearness induced by concentration on Him. In *mahabba,* the Sufi loses himself in awareness of his beloved. Among the fruits of mahabba are visions and the "station of unity," where zikr (the remembrance), *zakir* (the one who remembers), and *mazkur* (the one remembered) become one. A Theravadan Buddhist might see these experiences as entry into first jhana. Sufis recognize mastery at the point when the zakir's attention fixes on the zikr without effort, driving out other thoughts from his mind. Sufis see this state, called *fana,* as a pure gift of grace in which the zakir is "lost in Truth." Fana means "passing away in God." It is attained, notes Arberry (1972), when "self as well as the world has been cast aside." The cessation of both internal and external awareness in one-pointed focus on the zikr marks the Sufi's absorption of fana as comparable to the Buddhist's jhana.

Practice in the Sufi way extends to every waking moment, as is evident in directions for one technique of a proto-Sufi order (Bennett, 1973: p. 34): "Be present at every breath. Do not let your attention wander for the duration of a single breath. Remember yourself always and in all situations." The extension of practice to all situations culminates in *baqa,* abiding in some degree of fana consciousness while in the midst of ordinary activity. The tenth-century Sufi al-Junaid of Baghdad gives a classic definition of fana as "dying-to-self," which carries over as baqa, "life-in-Him." In this transition, the Sufi does not cease to function as an individual; rather, his nature becomes perfected. The Sufi Idries Shah (1971) speaks of this change in terms of an "extra dimension of being" operating parallel to ordinary cognition and calls it "objective consciousness." Others speak of an inner transformation wherein the Sufi acquires "reflexes that conform to spiritual reality."

Sufis insist that their teaching must never be fixedly dogmatic but flexible enough to fit the needs of specific persons, times, and places. As one modern teacher, Sufi Abdul-Hamid, puts it (Shah, 1972: p. 60): "The Work is carried out by the teacher in accordance with his perception of the situation in which he finds himself. This means that there is no textbook, no system, no method, other than that which belongs to the school of the moment." There have been many guidebooks prepared for the Sufi seeker in different times and places. One such is Abu al-Najib's (1975) twelfth-century *A Sufi Rule for Novices,* a classical manual of the Sufi path. Though this Sufi rule may bear little resemblance to contemporary practice, it allows us useful glimpses into the specifics of Sufi method and instructive comparisons to other spiritual paths.

Ibn al-Najib (A.D. 1097–1168) set down his rules for conduct for beginners in the Suhrwardi order to which he belonged; its purpose is comparable to that of the Visuddhimagga. Though these rules pertain to a certain group in a specific time and place, they have been used throughout the Muslim world and are themselves the basis for later Sufi instructional works. These rules give one of many variations on Sufi training. Many rules resonate with advice to Buddhist, Hindu, Kabbalist, and early Christian seekers. Just as the Bhakti is told to keep to satsang, al-Muridin advises: "The Sufi should associate with people of his kind and those from whom he can benefit." The novice should attach himself to a qualified teacher, or *shayk,* constantly seeking his direction and obeying him fully. He is urged to render service to his shayk and his fellows. Service is exalted as the best calling for the aspirant; the servant is said to rank next to the shayk himself. As in the Visuddhimagga and Christ's Sermon on the Mount, the novice's rules dictate: "One should not be concerned about the provisions of livelihood nor should one be occupied in seeking, gathering and storing them." For the Prophet himself "did not store anything for the morrow." Coveting food, clothes, or shelter hinders the Sufi's purity, for God revealed: "Those hearts which were bound to their desires were screened from Him." Though celibacy is not required of Sufis, these twelfth-century rules adjure: "In our times it is better to avoid marriage and suppress desire by discipline, hunger, vigils, and traveling." Finally, the Sufi must be a Moslem par excellence, observing all rules of the faith to the letter, for "the more saintly the man, the more strictly will he be judged."

Each Sufi master, order, and group has its own methods or combination of teaching techniques. The ways vary, but the goal is the same. Mahmud Shabastri, a master and author of *The Secret Garden,* put it this way:

> That man attains to the secret of unity
> Who is not detained at the stages on the road.
> Your being is naught but thorns and weeds,

Cast it all clean away from you.
Go sweep out the chamber of your heart,
Make it ready to be the dwelling place of the Beloved.
When you depart out, He will enter in,
In you, void of yourself, will He display His beauty.

Sufi doctrine holds men are bound by their conditioning—the thorns and weeds that keep them from God. The
ordinary man is trapped in suffering by his conditioning.
Strong habits of thought, feeling, and perception dictate
human reactions to the world; man is a slave to his habits.
People are asleep but do not know it. To awaken them to
their condition—the first step in escaping it—people need
a shock. One function of Sufi teaching stories, such as the
tale of the blind men and the elephant, is to provide such
a shock. These tales have many layers of meaning. Some are
hidden to most hearers, some obvious. Not everyone gets the
same lessons from the stories, for what the listener hears
depends on his stage along the Sufi path. The skillful teacher
uses just the right tale at the perfect moment to impart an
understanding for which the student is ripe.

Such shocks and lessons all help the Sufi aspirant on his
way to inner purification. According to Sufi psychology,
our habitual impulses are the stuff of the lower soul, or *nafs,*
which must be disciplined and watched continually lest it
lead the seeker toward evil and away from God. Al-Muridin
recommends overcoming the influence of nafs by detached
observation of its workings. Nafs, goes a saying, are like an
idol; looking at it with sympathy is idolatry; looking with
scrutiny is worship. Through detached scrutiny of his lower
urges, impulses, and desires, the Sufi can break their hold
over his mind and so replace his negative qualities with
virtuous ones.

Al-Muridin comments in his rules that "the consummate

Sufi is in a position of stability, and he is immune to the effects of the changeful states of mind or harsh circumstances." This equanimity allows the finished Sufi to be in the world but not of it. A calm exterior, however, may not reflect the inner ecstasy of a close communion with God. One modern shayk describes the Sufi's supreme state as "being inwardly drunk and outwardly sober."

One old master includes in his list of the finished Sufi's attributes: a sense of being subject entirely to God rather than one's own will; the desire to have no personal desire; "grace"—that is, perfect performance of acts in God's service; truthfulness in thought and deed; putting others' interests before one's own; service with complete self-disregard; constant remembrance of God; generosity, fearlessness, and the ability to die nobly. But Sufis may balk at such specific formulae for measuring spiritual progress, or worse, at trying to gauge another's attainments through such a checklist.

Those who would judge others should heed the advice in a Sufi tale retold by Idries Shah (1971: p. 75):

> Yaqub, the son of the Judge, said that one day he questioned Bahaudin Nawshband in this manner: When I was in companionship with the Murshid of Tabriz, he regularly made a sign that he was not to be spoken to, when he was in a condition of special reflection. But you are accessible to us at all times. Am I correct in concluding that this difference is due to your undoubtedly greater capacity of detachment, the capacity being under your dominion, rather than fugitive? Bahaudin told him:
> No, you are always seeking comparisons between people and between states. You are always seeking evidences and differences, when you are not you are seeking similarities. You do not really need so much

explanation in matters which are outside such measurement. Different modes of behavior on the part of the wise are to be regarded as due to differences in individuality; not of quality.

8. TRANSCENDENTAL MEDITATION

Transcendental Meditation (TM) is the best-known meditation technique in the West and Maharishi Mahesh Yogi, its formulator, the most famous yogi. TM is a classic Hindu mantra meditation in a modern Western package. Maharishi has been artful in his avoidance of Sanskrit terms and use of scientific findings to validate meditation in a skeptical culture so that normal Americans can feel comfortable joining in a practice developed by and for Hindus in India. He also downplays the orthodox nature of his beliefs. The theory behind TM—"Science of Creative Intelligence"—is an updated restatement of the basic teaching of Sankaracharya's eighth-century Advait school of Vedantic thought.

Sankaracharya wrote at a time when Buddhism dominated India. His highly successful religious crusade revived Hinduism, offering a final state of nonduality rather than nirvana to the seeker. The goal of Advait is union of the seeker's mind with the formless Brahma or infinite consciousness, a step beyond the Bhakti's goal of union with a form of God. The means to this formless union is samadhi. This is also the goal in TM, though Maharishi no longer describes it in these terms. TM traces its root back to San-

karacharya, though it is a reformulation of Advait thought
tailored to Western ears.

Maharishi's technique of TM is in the mainstream of jhana
practices, though it is often touted as unique. Like all Advait
yogis, Maharishi sees that "duality is the fundamental cause
of suffering." His technique for transcending duality begins
with repetition of a mantra, a Sanskrit word or sound. Just
as in the Visuddhimagga, in which different meditation
subjects are given to people of different temperament,
Maharishi claims that selection of the proper mantra for a
particular individual is a vital factor in TM. And just as the
Visuddhimagga depicts finer levels of one-pointedness as
increasingly blissful and sublime, Maharishi describes the
increasing "charm" as the mind is allowed to follow its
natural tendency to go to "a field of greater happiness" by
entering the subtler states of a thought—that is, the mantra.

There is a mystique about the specialness of each person's
mantra, and teachers admonish newcomers never to reveal
theirs to anyone or even speak it aloud. But as meditators
are sometimes chagrined to learn, people who fall into general categories of age, education, and so on, are given the
same mantra. The mantras themselves are by no means special to TM but come from standard Sanskrit sources used by
many Hindus today. Like millions of modern Bhaktis in
India, the TM meditator in Des Moines may be silently
intoning "Shyam" (a name of Lord Krishna), or "Aing" (a
sound sacred to the Divine Mother).

The beliefs that particular mantric sounds bestow certain
boons or are appropriate to special types of persons is widespread in Hinduism. The ancient *Saiva Upanishads,* for example, contain a discourse on the fifty letters of the Sanskrit
alphabet, treating each as a mantra in itself and describing
its special virtues. The letter *umkara* (Ū) gives strength;

kumkara (kā) is an antidote against poisons; *ghamkara* (gha) bestows prosperity; *phamkara* (pha) grants psychic powers.

In TM, meditators learn to avoid effortful concentration. The student is told to bring his mind gently back to the mantra as it wanders. In effect, this process is one of becoming one-pointed, though concentration is passive rather than forced. The following oft-quoted description by Maharishi (1969: p. 470) of the nature of TM well describes the focal narrowing of attention on a meditation object, and transcendence of the object, in ascending through access concentration to the second jhana. Transcendental meditation, he says, entails ". . . turning the attention inward towards the subtler levels of a thought until the mind transcends the experience of the subtlest state of the thought and arrives at the source of thought . . ."

As in the jhanas, bliss arises with the stillness of mind. The goal of mantra is what Maharishi calls "transcendental consciousness": when mind "arrives at the direct experience of bliss, it loses all contact with the outside and is contented in the state of transcendental bliss-consciousness." In the language of the Visuddhimagga, this is access concentration or jhana. The next phase in Maharishi's program is the infusion of jhana, or transcendental consciousness, into the waking, dreaming, and sleeping states by alternating normal activity with periods of meditation. The state thereby achieved he calls "cosmic consciousness" in which "no activity, however rigorous, can take one out of Being." Maharishi denies the need to impose renunciation on oneself. He sees purification as part of cosmic consciousness. It is an effect of transcendence, not a prerequisite. According to Maharishi, "Proficiency in the virtues can only be gained by repeated experience of samadhi."

Before the meditator gains cosmic consciousness, the effects of his daily meditation gradually wear off as time passes; in cosmic consciousness, these effects persist always. Maharishi elaborates the transition from transcendental to cosmic consciousness (1966: p. 53):

> From this state of pure Being the mind comes back again to experience the thought in the relative world. . . . With more and more practice, the ability of the mind to maintain its essential nature while experiencing objects through the senses increases. When this happens the mind and its essential nature, the state of transcendental Being, become one, and the mind is then capable of retaining its essential nature—Being—while engaged in thought, speech or action.

He sees cosmic consciousness as a state in which two distinct levels of organization in nervous system function. Usually, these levels inhibit each other, but here they operate side by side while they maintain their unique characteristics: Transcendental consciousness, for example, co-exists with the waking state. "Silence," says Maharishi, "is experienced with activity and yet is separate from it." The meditator in cosmic consciousness finds this inner peace persists in all circumstances as a "pure awareness" along with activity. Although the effects of transcendence during meditation can wear off after meditation is over, once mastered, cosmic consciousness is permanent. The person in cosmic consciousness has experienced in transcendence a jhanic state in which sense perception ceases. During waking, he remains relatively detached from sense perception, although he is more sensitive to both his own thought processes and external events.

As cosmic consciousness deepens, the meditator finds the bliss of transcendental consciousness persisting now in other states. As this bliss pervades other areas of his life, he finds that by comparison sensual pleasures are not so enchanting as before. While he still has desires, his actions are no longer driven by them. His state is one of equanimity: The turbulence and excitement of intense emotions—fear, grief, anger, depression, or craving—are softened by a permanent state of "restful alertness." Finally, they cease to arise. Equanimity also shows up in the meditator better resisting the fluctuating pull of life stress and daily tensions. He finds a new inner steadiness prevails, whereas once he would have wavered. Even-mindedness also manifests in the meditator loving others in equal share without undue fondness for specific people; his attachments weaken. He also finds he is more easily contented with whatever comes, more free from desires and dislikes. According to Maharishi, life in cosmic consciousness is tensionless (1969: p. 287):

> The enlightened man lives a life of fulfillment. His actions, being free from desire, serve only the need of the time. He has no personal interest to gain. He is engaged in fulfilling the cosmic purpose and therefore his actions are guided by nature. This is why he does not have to worry about his needs. His needs are the needs of nature, which takes care of their fulfillment, he being the instrument of the Divine.

A further step in the progression promised by Maharishi is God consciousness. This state is the result of devotion while in cosmic consciousness. In "God consciousness" the meditator perceives all things as sacred; "everything is naturally experienced in the awareness of God." At first, says Maharishi, this experience of unity in diversity can be overwhelming, and the meditator can become deeply lost in it. Gradually, however, God consciousness mixes with other activities, just as at an earlier stage transcendental consciousness merged with normal states to produce cosmic consciousness.

In God consciousness the meditator surrenders his individuality. This is "the most purified state" in which the meditator has overcome the least stain of impurity in thought or deed; he now dwells in perfect harmony with nature and the divine. Arriving at God consciousness, according to Maharishi, entails a transformation, whereby one is aware of God in all aspects of creation. Beyond God consciousness the TM devotee may evolve into a state called "unity." Here his consciousness is so refined that he perceives all things free of any conceptual illusion.

The means to these higher states in TM are advanced techniques given to meditators over the course of several years of practice and of service to the TM organization. The advanced TM siddhis course seeks to expand the meditator's range by developing unusual powers, such as the ability to "levitate." The classical basis for using meditation to cultivate "supernormal" abilities is discussed in the next section.

9. PATANJALI'S ASHTANGA YOGA

The manual for meditators closest to the Visuddhimagga in Hinduism is Patanjali's *Yoga Sutras,* still the most authoritative source on yoga today (Prabhavananda and Isherwood, 1969; Vivekananda, 1970). Most every modern Indian meditation system, including TM, acknowledges the Yoga Sutras as one source of their own method. There are numerous spiritual schools called "yoga": Bhakti yoga is the path of devotion; karma yoga uses selfless service; and gyana yoga takes the intellect as its vehicle. The path outlined in the Yoga Sutras subsumes them all.

Though their means may differ, all yogic paths seek to transcend duality in union. All these paths see the locus of duality as within the mind, in the separation between the mechanisms of awareness and their object. To transcend duality, the seeker must enter a state in which this gap is bridged, the experiencer and the object merging. This state is samadhi, in which the meditator's awareness merges with its contents.

The yoga aphorisms are a skeletal map to this state. The mind, it explains, is filled with thought waves that create the gulf that yoga seeks to bridge. By calming his thought waves, by stilling his mind, the yogi will find union. These thought waves are the source of strong emotions and blind habits that bind man to a false self. When his mind becomes clear and still, man can know himself as he really is. In this stillness, he can know God. In the process, his mistaken belief in himself as a separate, unique individual apart from God will be overcome. As his thought waves are subdued, the yogi's ego recedes. Finally, as a liberated man, he is able to don his ego or discard it like a suit of clothes. Donning the ego, he acts in the world; discarding it by stilling his mind, he unites with God.

But first he must undergo an arduous discipline of mind and body. This transformation begins with concentration, bringing his mind to one-pointedness. In Patanjali's system, one-pointedness is the main method around which all others turn. Some sources date the aphorisms back more than fifteen hundred years, to about the same period as the Visuddhimagga. The spiritual *Zeitgeist* of that era is reflected in both; indeed, the paths they outline are in large part identical. The main difference between these two meditation manuals is Patanjali's insistence that samadhi rather than nirvana is the highway to liberation.

The royal, or *raja,* yoga outlined by Patanjali entails *ashtanga:* eight key practices or limbs. The first two, *yama* and *niyama,* are moral training for purity. The next two are *asana,* the development through physical exercises of a firm and erect posture, or "seat," and *pranayam,* exercises for controlling and stilling the breath. Both the third and fourth limbs have become intricately developed in their own right, so that some yogic schools use these practices as their main methods—and most Americans associate "yoga" exclusively with these two limbs.

Most textbooks of *hatha* and pranayam point out that these are aids to the attainment of samadhi, not ends in themselves. Some, however, focus solely on rigorous physical purifications as means to alter consciousness. Vyas Dev (1970), for example, details 250 *asana* postures, elaborates fifty different pranayam exercises and twenty-five *shat-karmas* and *mudras*—methods for cleansing internal organs. Before sitting in deep meditation for a long time, advises Vyas Dev, the yogi should clear his bowels completely by drawing in and expelling water through his anus, empty his bladder by drawing in water and then expelling it through a catheter, and purify his digestive system by swallowing and extracting about seventy feet of string made of fine yarn. He should also swallow two or three pints of lukewarm salt water to make himself vomit and swallow and extract a three-inch-wide strip of cloth seven yards long to finish the job. Then he is ready for serious meditation.

Patanjali's stipulation about these first four limbs, however, is that the yogi should do them simply to the point at which his body and mind are stilled. These are mere preliminaries for sitting in meditation, useful for overcoming the obstacles to concentration such as doubt, sloth, de-

spair, and craving for sensual pleasures. Actual meditation
begins with the second group of limbs. These are all steps
in becoming one-pointed. In the fifth limb, *pratyahara,* the
yogi withdraws his mind from sense objects, focusing his
attention on the meditation object. In the sixth, *dharana,* he
holds his mind on the object. The seventh, *dhyana,* involves
"an unbroken flow of thought toward the object of concentration." The sixth and seventh limbs correspond to initial
and sustained application of attention in the Visuddhimagga
system. The final limb is samadhi.

The combination dharana, dhyana, and samadhi is a state
called *samyama.* This highly concentrated state holds the key
to supernormal powers such as clairvoyance and telepathy.
The Sutras have a lengthy section on how to apply samyama
to gain various powers. By focusing samyama on his memories, the yogi can retrieve knowledge of his past lives;
samyama on the marks of another's body reveals his state of
mind; samyama on the yogi's own throat stills his hunger
and thirst. As in the Visuddhimagga, the Sutras see these
powers as subtle snares for the seeker. The yogi is urged to
give up these seductive traps as last temptations for the ego.

The aphorisms say that samyama on "single moments and
their sequence" gives discriminative knowledge, or *prajna,*
which "delivers from the bondage of ignorance." But this
foray into the path of insight seems glossed over in most
modern commentaries on Patanjali. It is samadhi that is
taught as the heart of yoga; Vivekananda (1970) says,
"Samadhi is Yoga proper; that is the highest means." Patanjali lists many suitable objects for concentration: the syllable
Om, or other mantra; the heart; a deity or "illumined soul";
or a divine symbol. The yogi, in merging consciousness with
the primary object, will first achieve savichara samadhi—
access concentration. In this level of samadhi, there is identity with the primary object "mixed with awareness of

name, quality, and knowledge." After this comes *nirvichara* samadhi—first jhana, in which there is identity without other awareness. Once the nirvichara level is gained, the yogi is to wipe out even the thought of the primary object and so attain *nirvikalpa* samadhi (as in the example of Sri Ramakrishna), in which all sense of duality is obliterated.

Nirvikalpa is the deepest samadhi; in it, mind is at its stillest. Yogic lore has it that one in this state could remain for as long as three months in continuous deep meditation, his breath and other metabolic functions virtually suspended all that time. In this samadhi, says one commentator, "an avalanche of indescribable bliss sweeps away all relative ideas of pain and blame . . . All doubts and misgivings are quelled forever; the oscillations of mind are stopped; the momentum of past actions is exhausted." But one limit of nirvikalpa samadhi is that it can be enjoyed only while the yogi remains still, absorbed in deep meditation.

The final step in ashtanga yoga is extending the deep stillness of samadhi into the yogi's waking state. When samadhi spreads throughout other states so that no activity or inner stirring can dislodge its hold on the yogi's mind, this marks him as a *jivan-mukti,* a liberated man. In his introduction to Sri Ramakrishna's biography, the anonymous chronicler gives an eloquent account of the state enjoyed by that saint (M., 1952: p. 27). On emerging from nirvikalpa samadhi:

> he is devoid of ideas of "I" and "mine," he looks on the body as a mere shadow, an outer sheath encasing the soul. He does not dwell on the past, takes no thought for the future, and looks with indifference on the present. He surveys everything in the world with an eye of equality; he is no longer touched by the infinite variety of phenomenon; he no longer reacts to

pleasure and pain. He remains unmoved where he—that is to say, his body—is worshipped by the good or tormented by the wicked; for he realizes that it is the one Brahman that manifests itself through everything.

The Indian saint Ramana Maharshi (1962) proposed a simple operational definition for distinguishing between a yogi in nirvikalpa samadhi and one in sahaj samadhi: If there remains a difference between samadhi and the waking state, it is nirvikalpa samadhi at best; if no difference, the yogi has reached his goal of sahaj samadhi.

The yogi in sahaj partially resides in samadhi, no longer identifying with his thoughts or senses. His being is grounded in a consciousness transcending the sensory world, and so he remains detached from that world while operating in it. This "ideal of Yoga, the state of *jivan-mukti,*" writes Eliade (1970), is life in an "eternal present" in which one "no longer possesses a personal consciousness—that is, a consciousness nourished on his own history—but a witness consciousness which is pure lucidity and spontaneity."

In sahaj samadhi, meditation is a self-sustained, spontaneous fact of the yogi's existence. He expresses his stillness of mind in his actions. He is free of all ego ties and interests; his actions are no longer bound by the deposits of the past. Meher Baba (1967) describes this as "a state of full wakefulness in which there is no ebb and flow, waxing or waning, but only the steadiness of true perception." The jivan-mukti has transcended his body consciousness along with the conceptual universe; he does not see the world as different from himself. For one who dwells in sahaj, there is no ego, and there are no "others."

10. INDIAN TANTRA
AND KUNDALINI YOGA

The Tantric tradition native to India is, according to some sources, a refinement of ancient shamanistic practices that has found its way into both Hindu and Buddhist meditation systems (Eliade, 1970). Indian Tantra alters consciousness by arousing energies that are normally latent. Some meditation systems introduced to the West have their roots in "kundalini" yoga, a Tantric teaching. Kundalini, says Tantric physiology, is a huge reserve of spiritual energy located at the base of the spine. When aroused, kundalini travels up the spine through six centers, or *"chakras,"* reaching the seventh at the top of the head. Kundalini has few specific correlates with Western notions of anatomy. Chakras refer to energy patterns, localized in certain non-physical centers.

When kundalini focuses in a chakra, it activates characteristic energies of these centers. Each chakra has an emblematic set of attitudes, motives, and mental states that dominate a person's mind when kundalini sparks it. The first chakra, located between the anus and the genitals, involves the struggle to survive. Territoriality, possessiveness, brute force, undue preoccupation with the body and health, and fear for one's safety all reflect the mental state of the first chakra. The second chakra embodies sexuality and sensuality. It is in the genitals. When this chakra is active, lust, greed, and craving for sensual delights are one's predominant states of mind. The urge to be powerful and influence others is tied to the third chakra, located near the navel. Persuasion or manipulation of others to serve one's own ends are third-chakra behavior.

Most people much of the time are motivated by mental

states in which these first three chakras are active. Kundalini yoga aims to bring this energy up to the higher chakras, just as Kabbalah seeks to raise consciousness to higher planes. The fourth chakra, in the center of the chest by the heart, represents selfless love and caring for others. The pure love of a mother for her child is of the fourth chakra. But fourth-chakra love is not romantic; rather, it combines with a clear-sighted detachment to make for compassion. When kundalini activates the three topmost chakras, the yogi experiences transcendental states. These three centers are the fifth chakra at the throat, the sixth at the center of the forehead, and the seventh at the top of the head. The meditator seeks to free kundalini from his lower chakras, in which it ordinarily is trapped, and raise it to his higher ones. When it reaches his seventh chakra and stabilizes there, he feels a state of intense ecstasy and union with God. He is considered liberated, free of bondage to those habits and acts stemming from the lower chakras by which most men are bound.

The essence of Tantric practice is the use of the senses to transcend sense consciousness in samadhi. Though the senses are, of course, the means to transcendence in all techniques for one-pointedness, Tantrism is unique in the diversity of techniques it offers for transcending sense consciousness. Among them are the use of mantra; *yantra,* objects for visualization exercises such as a mandala; concentration on *shabd,* supersubtle inner sounds; pranayam and asanas; concentration on the play of forces in the chakras; and *maithuna,* the arousal of *shakti*—kundalini energy—through controlled, ritual sexual intercourse.

Maithuna is the Tantric technique that most fascinates Westerners, who more often than not mistake it for an indulgence of sexual appetites rather than a means to their mastery. Ritual intercourse is a potent means to arouse kundalini energy, allowing the self-disciplined yogi to raise this energy to his higher chakras. Maithuna is one of five actions generally prohibited to Hindu yogis but used by Tantrics of the Bon Marg, or "left-handed path." The first four are imbibing fish, meat, liquor, and performing certain mudras, all of which the Tantric does in a strictly prescribed manner, as a prelude to maithuna. Throughout the ritual, he does silent japa of his own special mantra, given by his guru, and at points he recites certain other mantras. During maithuna itself, the yogi carries out carefully delineated ritual actions—including exactly where and how to touch his partner's body.

In maithuna, the male is passive, the female active; since the arousal of energy rather than climax is the goal, there is little movement. During intercourse, the Tantric mentally recites mantras such as "Om, thou goddess resplendent . . . into the fire of the self, using the mind as a sacrificial ladle, I, who am engaged in harnessing the sense organs, offer this oblation." At the moment of ejaculation, he is to repeat a mantra that consecrates his semen itself as a sacrificial offering (Bharati, 1970). The key to maithuna, as well as the goal of all Tantric practices, is the detachment borne of samadhi. This detachment converts the energy of desires into higher forms. Tantric texts frequently repeat (Eliade, 1970: p. 263): "By the same acts that cause some men to burn in hell for thousands of years, the Yogin gains his eternal salvation."

Tantric language is veiled and so is open to many levels of interpretation. Actions that from outside seem improper can have within Tantra a special, deeper meaning. An example of this double meaning in Tantra is a Tibetan *kapala*, a cup made of human skull mounted on a silver stand. Its description in a museum reads:

The vessel holds the Amrit used for performing esoteric
rituals. Those who have such dualistic concepts as the
clean and the unclean cannot think of using a human
skull. But the Tantrics, who have gained Transcendental Wisdom, have no superstition and to them golden
cups and human skulls are the same. The skulls are used
to symbolize this attitude of mind.

One modern version of kundalini yoga is *siddha-yoga,*
taught by the late Swami Muktananda (Amma, 1969; Muktananda, 1969). This system begins with traditional practices
such as asana, pranayam, chanting, and japa. He instructs the
beginner to meditate with the mantra, "Guru Om," or with
each breath, "so-ham." Muktananda emphasizes the guru-
disciple relationships. The core of siddha-yoga training is the
tradition in which the guru grants a direct, instantaneous
transcendental experience to the devotee. This process, called
shaktipat diksha, is an initiation by look, touch, or word. In
this transmission the devotee who approaches the guru with
love, devotion, and faith has his shakti—the energy of kundalini—aroused.

When this happens, all other practices can fall away. The
inner action of kundalini produces spontaneous meditation,
pranayam, asanas, and mudras without the devotee's prior
training or volition. This process of purification through
shaktipat is said to take three to twelve years. In this period
it transforms the entire personality of the devotee, the "limited I" having been abandoned. The devotee attains a sense
of "oneness with all-pervading Cosmic Intellect." The im-
agery and terminology with which Muktananda describes
this process is that of kundalini (1970: p. 54):

The Kundalini, which stays in the *Muladhara* [first
chakra], gradually travels upwards piercing the chakras

on her way until she reaches *Sahasrara* [seventh chakra], the thousand-petalled lotus in the crown of the head . . . and the spiritual endeavor of an aspirant gets fulfilled.

During shaktipat the meditator may experience a wide variety of involuntary reactions. These include powerful moods of joy, dullness, or agitation; strange bodily postures, gestures, tremors, or dancing poses; feelings of wonder or fright; a period of pain in all parts of the body; various internal stirrings, muscle throbbing, or thrills; spontaneous deep meditation; visions of lights, deities, or celestial places accompanied by a great joy and bliss; and, finally, there is a "divine light of indescribable lustre" or a subtle inner sound during meditation (Muktananda, 1970).

These phenomena serve to purify the meditator so that he can sustain *turiya*—a state akin to jhana—while in the three ordinary states of waking, dreaming, and sleeping. He reaches the further state of *Turiyatita* when his kundalini has stabilized in the topmost chakra, the *sahasrara.* A person in this advanced state has forgotten body consciousness, enjoys extraordinary bliss and profound tranquility, and has attained "the fruit of Yoga," remaining "ever absorbed in the Supreme State," whatever he does. He performs any and all acts with peace and equanimity. A disciple of Muktananda, Amma (1969: p. 11), says of one in this state, "He has nothing to do and nothing to achieve; still he does the activities of worldly life remaining a witness to them all." One in turiyatita has become a siddha, a name denoting the supernormal psychic powers he is said to possess, among which is the capability of raising kundalini in others.

Tantra yoga is one of the few traditional meditation systems that sees the yogi's attainment of siddhis, or supernormal psychic powers, as marking the end of his path. Says one Tantric scripture, "For all sadhana ceases when it has borne its fruit in siddhi." Certain Tantric practices are devised to produce certain siddhis such as mind reading. One reason siddhis may signify liberation for some is the high states that the possession of powers signifies. But meditation is central to all Tantric practices; the raising of kundalini, the means; samadhi, the goal.

11. TIBETAN BUDDHISM

The techniques of Tibetan Mahayana are founded in the classical Buddhist tradition that the Visuddhimagga expresses. It also blends with the classical, purely Tibetan elements and Tantraism. In an outline of meditation theory and practice by the Dalai Lama (1965), the theory presented is essentially that of the Theravadan Visuddhimagga—or as Mahayanists call Theravada, the "Hinayana" tradition, or "Lesser Vehicle," in contrast to their "Greater Vehicle." A critical difference between these two main Buddhist traditions is the Mahayana bodhisattva vow to gain enlightenment not just for oneself but for the sake of the salvation of all sentient beings. This difference in motive, says the Dalai Lama, is decisive; it makes a difference in both path and goal. He sees the hinayana nirvana as a prior stage to the Mahayana goal of bodhisattvahood. Still, his conception of the nirvanic state agrees with the Visuddhimagga: it is "liberation from this bondage" of *samsara* by a cessation in which the "roots of delusion are thoroughly extracted," the ego or "I-thought" severed. But for Mahayanists the goal is beyond nirvana, in returning to the world and helping others toward salvation.

Motive determines the outcome of insight into emptiness. If he developed insight solely to liberate himself, he will be what, as we have seen earlier, the Visuddhimagga calls an *arahant.* If he was motivated by the "Bodhi-chitta of love and compassion," he gains the "superior release" of the bodhisattva, in which his state of consciousness makes him a more perfect vehicle of compassion so he can lead others toward liberation. In either case, says the Dalai Lama, a bodhisattva has "cleansed his mind of all impurities and has removed the motives and inclinations that lead to them." He has severed ties to the normal world of name and form, the locus of ordinary consciousness.

The Mahayana path begins with a close cousin of the Visuddhimagga teaching. There are three "moral precepts," ways for the meditator to realize the "Triple Refuge"— Buddha, Dharma, and Sangha—as his internal realities. The Tibetan Buddhist meditator's first precept is *sila,* vows of upright behavior. The second is samadhi (Tibetan: *shiney*), fixing the mind on one object to develop his one-pointedness. The recommended conditions in which to practice samadhi are as in the Visuddhimagga. The meditator should go into seclusion, sever his ties to worldly activities, and so on. The early meditation objects include those listed in the Visuddhimagga, such as mindfulness of the breath. Some, especially in later stages, resemble Indian Tantric deities. These more advanced subjects are the object of visualization. Such subjects come in innumerable aspects "so that they suit the physical, mental and sensuous attitudes of different individuals," and arouse strong faith and devotion. These visualization subjects embody different aspects of the mind. The meditator identifies with these mental states or qualities as he visualizes the figure. Chogyam Trungpa (1975: p. 47) describes one such figure:

> On the disc of the autumn moon, clear and pure, you place a seed syllable. The cool blue rays of the seed syllable emanate immense cooling compassion that radiates beyond the limits of sky or space. It fulfills the needs and desires of sentient beings, bringing basic warmth so that confusions may be clarified. Then from the seed syllable you create a Mahavairocana Buddha, white in color, with the features of an aristocrat—an eight-year-old child with a beautiful, innocent, pure, powerful, royal gaze. He is dressed in the costume of a medieval king of India. He wears a glittering gold crown inlaid with wishfulfilling jewels. Part of his long black hair floats over his shoulders and back; the rest is made into a topknot surmounted by a glittering blue diamond. He is seated crosslegged on the lunar disc with his hands in the meditation mudra holding a vajra carved from pure white crystal.

The Dalai Lama lists four steps in reaching samadhi. There is an initial fixing of the meditator's mind on the primary object while he tries to prolong his period of concentration on it. In the next stage, his concentration is intermittent. Distractions come and go in his mind, alternating with attention to the primary object. At this stage, he may experience joy and ecstasy arising from his one-pointedness; these feelings will strengthen his efforts at concentration. This stage, like jhana access, culminates when his mind finally overcomes all disturbances, enabling him to concentrate on the object without any interruption whatsoever in the perfect one-pointedness of the jhanas. The final stage is that of "mental quiescence," in which his total concentration comes with minimal effort—that is, jhana mastery. The meditator can now concentrate on any object with effortless ease; psychic powers have become possible.

Jhana mastery matters in Mahayana not because of the powers made possible but due to its usefulness in the meditator's realizing *Sunyata,* the essential emptiness of the phenomenal world, including the world within the meditator's own mind. The means for this breakthrough is the meditator's third precept, the practice of vipassana (Tibetan: *thagthong*). He uses the power of samadhi as a steppingstone for meditation on Sunyata. The Dalai Lama (1965) does not specify details of vipassana technique in Tibetan practice. But he does mention that the flow of the meditator's undisciplined mind can be stopped "and the wandering or projecting mind brought to rest by concentration on the physical makeup of one's body and the psychological makeup of one's mind"—two techniques of vipassana taught in the Visuddhimagga. By means of vipassana with Sunyata as focus, the meditator discards his ego beliefs, finally reaching "the goal that leads to the destruction of all moral and mental defilements."

This goal does not, however, represent the culmination of the meditator's spiritual development in Tibetan Buddhism but a stage along the way in his further practice and evolution. The control of mental processes he gains through concentration and insight prepare him for further training in techniques such as visualizations and the cultivation of qualities such as compassion. The many schools within Tibetan Buddhism have their particular emphasis and unique program for advanced training. In all of them, the basic meditative skills of concentration and insight are prerequisites for more complex, advanced efforts in training the meditator's mind.

Chogyam Trungpa (1976), in summarizing the Tibetan

Buddhist path, advises that before the meditator begins any advanced Tibetan techniques, he needs to develop "transcendental common sense, seeing things as they are." For this reason, vipassana meditation forms the meditator's foundation. With seeing things clearly, the meditator relaxes his defenses in daily living situation. This opens him to *shunyata,* "direct experience without any props." This, in turn, inspires the meditator to aim toward the bodhisattva ideal. But this is not the end of the path: Beyond the bodhisattva experience is that of the "yogi," beyond the yogi is the "siddha," and beyond the siddha lies the "Buddha." At each of these levels, the seeker has a unique sense of himself and the world—for example, the bodhisattva experiences shunyata. At a still higher level is the psychological space of *mahamudra.* Here, says Trungpa (Guenther and Trungpa, 1975: p. 36), "symbols do not exist as such; the sense of experience ceases to exist. Directly relating to the play of situations, energy develops through a movement of spontaneity that never becomes frivolous." This leads one to "destroy whatever needs to be destroyed, and foster whatever needs to be fostered." When one has arrived at mahamudra, there is no more struggling along the path.

It is difficult for someone to assess the true nature of any spiritual path without himself participating in its practices. This applies all the more to systems like Tibetan Buddhism in which the heart of instruction is esoteric. Vajrayana, the tantric segment of Tibetan Buddhism, is veiled in secrecy; the great legendary tantric Milarepa warns (Chang, 1970): "The teachings of Tantra should be practiced secretly; they will be lost if demonstrated in the marketplace." Even if told publicly, many Tibetan methods are "self-secret" so that one needs to practice them and experience their fruits truly to understand them. Translations like Evans-Wentz' (1968, 1969) give the reader a vivid taste of Tibetan teachings. But to follow this intricate path, one needs to find a lama as guru, for even now specific methods in Tibetan Buddhism are transmitted only from teacher to student in teaching lineages that date back centuries.

12. ZEN

The word "Zen" is a cognate of the Pali word *jhana*, and both derive from the Sanskrit dhyana (meditation). The cultural interchange that culminated in Japanese Zen links to the Visuddhimagga tradition through the Ch'an meditation school of China. The changes undergone in the voyage through time and space from India of the fifth century to Japan of the present day are more evident in doctrine than in the specifics of practice. Doctrinal differences—much like those between Theravada and Mahayana Buddhism—have emphasized these changes and obscured the similarities. Some versions of Zen meditation, or *zazen,* remain identical to mindfulness or insight. As with mindfulness, all varieties of zazen broaden their focus from sitting meditation to the meditator's whole range of life situations.

Zen's down-to-earth zazen matters, but extensive scriptural studies are discouraged. The early Soto master Dogen (1971: p. 62) stated:

No matter how well you say you know ... the esoteric and exoteric doctrines, as long as you possess a mind that clings to the body, you will be vainly counting others' treasures, without gaining even half a cent for yourself.

Zazen begins, as does vipassana, with a firm grounding in concentration; a wide variety of concentration techniques are employed. Samadhi or jhana is, in Zen terminology, the "great fixation" or "a state of oneness" in which the differences between things dissolve so that they appear to the meditator in the aspect of sameness. This is an intermediate stage on the path toward Zen's final realization. Suzuki warns (1958: p. 135): "When this state of great fixation is held as final, there will be no upturning, no outburst of satori, no penetration, no insight into Reality, no severing the bonds of birth and death." Deep absorptions are not enough. They are necessary but not sufficient steps toward enlightenment. The wisdom of insight follows after and flows from samadhi.

Among Zen techniques are some unique methods for achieving jhana. One such, the *koan* (used primarily by the Rinzai sect), is a puzzle utterly impervious to solution by reason. Its "solution" lies in transcending thought by liberating the meditator's mind from the snare of language (Miura and Sasaki, 1965). Assigned a koan such as "What was your face before you were born?" or "What is Mu?" the aspirant keeps the koan constantly in mind. No matter what he is doing, when other matters intrude on his mind, he immediately lets them go and returns to his koan. As he discovers that his rational mind is unable to solve the insoluble, he reaches a feverish pitch of concentration from which arises a supreme frustration. As this happens, what once was a fully stated koan reduces to an emblematic fragment, for example, simply "Mu." When his discursive faculty finally exhausts itself, the moment of "realization" comes to the meditator. His thought ceases and he enters the state of *daigi,* or "fixation." His koan "yields up all its secrets" as he attains samadhi. (Suzuki, 1958).

Yasutani, a modern roshi who came to teach in America,

utilized the koan for his more advanced students. He assigned beginners concentration on breathing. He saw as the aim of zazen not rendering the mind inactive in jhana but "quieting and unifying it in the midst of activity." Consequently, his students practiced concentration techniques until they developed a modicum of *joriki,* mental strength arising from one-pointedness of mind. The fruits of joriki are equanimity, determination, and a potential ripeness in the student for *Kensho-godo,* the *satori* awakening of "seeing into your True-nature." When the student uses a koan, for instance, his samadhi comes to fruition when there is "absolute unity with Mu, unthinking absorption in Mu—this is ripeness." At this point, "inside and outside merge into a single unity." With this samadhi experience, *Kensho-godo* can take place, where he will "see each thing just as it is." A given *kensho* experience may fall anywhere within a wide range of depth, degree, and clarity.

Joriki strengthens the meditator's satori. This helps him extend his awakening beyond the session of zazen per se. The joriki he develops in his zazen cultivates the satori effect until finally it shapes all the rest of his daily life. When the student gains some control over his mind via one-pointedness exercises like counting breath or has exhausted his rational mind with koan, Yasutani-roshi frequently set him to a more advanced method called *shikan-taza,* "just sitting." In this type of Zen meditation, the student marshals a heightened state of concentrated awareness with no primary object. He just sits, keenly aware of whatever goes on in and around him. He sits alert and mindful, free from points of view or discriminating thoughts, merely watching. This technique is quite similar to vipassana. A related practice is "mobile zazen," in which he enters fully into every action with total attention and clear awareness. This corresponds to "bare attention" as described in the Visuddhimagga. Kapleau

(1967) has noted these close parallels and cites a key Pali Sutra on mindfulness as a "prescription" for zazen:

> In what is seen there must be just the seen;
> In what is sensed there must be just the sensed;
> In what is thought there must be just the thought.

There are many kinds of "satori" in zazen practice, some of which may be experiences of jhana, some stages in the path of insight. Yasutani warns his students, for example, to ignore *makyo,* visions and intense sensations. He says these may arise when the student's ability to concentrate develops to a point within reach of kensho, just as similar phenomena may arise when the meditator approaches the access concentration level. Kapleau describes a "false satori" stage, sometimes called the "cave of Satan," in which the meditator experiences deep serenity and believes he has reached his final realization. Just as with the pseudonirvana on the vipassana path, this pseudoemancipation must be broken through. The final drive toward enlightenment as described by Kapleau (1967: p. 13) also fits the stages just prior to nirvana on the path of vipassana: The meditator's efforts are "powered on the one hand by a painfully felt inner bondage—a frustration with life, a fear of death, or both—and on the other by the conviction that through satori one can gain liberation." Yasutani notes that satori usually follows a period of samadhi. In an essay on his own Zen training, D. T. Suzuki says of his first attainment of samadhi, on the koan Mu (1970: p. 10):

> But this samadhi is not enough. You must come out of that state, be awakened from it and that awakening is prajna. That moment of coming out of samadhi and seeing it for what it is—that is satori.

Zen teachers stress the need to ripen an initial satori through further meditation until it finally permeates the meditator's whole life. Such full fruition means a state of mind stilled beyond any need for further practice. Suzuki (1949) describes this final state of mind as one in which the facts of one's daily experience are taken as they come; all events come into the meditator's awareness and are received with nonreaction. This nonreaction, clarifies Blofeld (1962), "does not mean trance-like dullness, but a brilliantly clear state of mind in which the details of every phenomenon are perceived, yet without evaluation or attachment."

Hui Hai, an old Zen master, put it, "When things happen, make no response: Keep your minds from dwelling on anything whatsoever." The fourteenth-century Zen master Bassui advised that zazen is "no more than looking into one's own mind, neither despising nor cherishing the thoughts that arise." This neutral stance is both means and end in Zen. It should extend beyond sitting in zazen into the rest of the meditator's day. Ruth Sasaki (Miura and Sasaki, 1965: p. xi) elaborates:

> The experienced practicer of zazen does not depend upon sitting in quietude on his cushion. States of consciousness at first attained only in the meditation hall gradually become continuous, regardless of what other activities he may be engaged in.

In the final Zen stage of "no mind," the spontaneous clarity of satori manifests in all one's acts. Here means and ends coalesce; the posture of mindfulness is built into the meditator's consciousness as a full awareness devoid of self-consciousness. Having experienced the impermanence of all things, that "life is pain, that all forms are *ku,* empty or voidness," he ceases clinging to the phenomenal world yet continues to act.

In recognition of the depth of this transformation of personality, there is little emphasis in Zen on moral precepts. Rather than merely imposing precepts from the outside, their observance emerges from within as a by-product of the change in consciousness zazen can bring. Thomas Merton (1965) points out that Zen teachings inherit the spirit of the Taoist Chuang Tzu, who wrote these words (p. 61):

> Minds free, thoughts gone,
> Brows clear, faces serene.
> All that came out of them
> Came quiet, like the four seasons.

13. GURDJIEFF'S FOURTH WAY

The spiritual system George I. Gurdjieff (1877–1948) brought to the West after extensive travel in Asia meeting "remarkable men" is, in the words of his pupil Orage, the religious teachings of the East disguised "in a terminology which would not alienate the factual minds of Western thinkers." Ouspensky (1971), another student of Gurdjieff, calls this system an "esoteric school," not suited to mass tastes, which tells *how* to do what popular religions teach *has* to be done, that is, transform one's consciousness. Gurdjieff himself called it "the Fourth Way": not the traditional path of the fakir, monk, or yogi but the way of the "sly

man" who does not retreat from the world in solitary meditation but works on his consciousness in the mirror of his
relationships with people, animals, property, and ideas. At
an advanced stage, the Gurdjieff student must share his acquired knowledge with others in order to advance still
further, so numerous second-, third-, and fourth-generation
Gurdjieff groups have developed, each with its own style
and idiosyncrasies. Since Gurdjieff's original school made
use of a great range of techniques, any given latter-day
group of his Fourth Way may or may not use the methods
discussed here, which are primarily Ouspensky's.

Gurdjieff says most people are "asleep," living a life of
automatic response to stimulus. "Contemporary man,"
writes Gurdjieff (1971), "has gradually deviated from the
natural type he ought to have represented . . . the perceptions
and manifestations of the modern man . . . represent only
the results of automatic reflexes of one or another part of
his general entirety." Like the Buddha, Gurdjieff understands man's normal state to be one of suffering. Human
beings, because we are unable to see the situation as it really
is, remain dominated by egoism, animal passions such as fear,
excitement, and anger, and the pursuit of pleasure. Suffering,
however, can give us an urge toward freedom. The way to
liberation is not by conventional notions of virtuous living
but by an intentional program for self-transformation. The
remedy Gurdjieff offers begins with self-observation.
Kenneth Walker (1969: p. 206), who studied with Ouspensky and Gurdjieff, puts it thus:

> We are imprisoned within our own minds, and how-
> ever far we extend them and however highly we deco-
> rate them we still remain within their walls. If we are
> ever to escape from our prisons, the first step must be

that we should realize our true situation and at the same
time see ourselves as we really are and not as we imag-
ine ourselves to be. This can be done by holding ourselves in a state of passive awareness . . .

Walker here describes "self-remembering," a technique of
deliberately dividing one's attention so as to direct a portion
back on oneself. Within one's multiple, fluctuating selves,
one establishes an awareness that only watches all the rest:
the "observing I" or the "witness." At first there is great
difficulty in coming to a stable observing I, the beginner
constantly forgets to remember himself, and self-observation
melts into his usual full identification with whichever "I"
has reign over his mind at a given moment. But with
persistence the beginner's self-remembering strengthens, for,
in Ouspensky's words, "the more we appreciate our present
psychological state of sleep, the more we appreciate the
urgent need to change it." Self-remembering is like mindfulness. The psychological stance required in this method is
self-directed detachment, as though one's own thoughts and
acts were those of some other person with whom one is only
slightly acquainted. Ouspensky (Walker, 1969: p. 40) instructs:

> Observe yourself very carefully and you will see that
> not *you* but *it* speaks within you, moves, feels, laughs,
> and cries in you, just as *it* rains, clears up and rains again
> outside you. Everything happens in you, and your first
> job is to observe and watch it happening.

When the student realizes there has been a lapse in his
self-observation, he returns his wandering mind to the task
of watching himself. Though various Gurdjieff circles use a
range of techniques, these are most often subsidiary to self-

remembering. The critical skill sought is the capacity to direct attention to self-observation. Ouspensky (1971) names both the samadhi trance state and the normal state of identifying that "imprisons man in some small part of himself" as antithetical to his goal. Just as with insight meditation, in self-remembering the "distorting glasses of the personality" are abandoned in order to see oneself clearly. In self-remembering, like mindfulness and zazen, one acknowledges oneself in entirety without comment and without naming what is seen.

Another example of Gurdjieffian self-remembering exercises is to focus on one aspect of everyday behavior—for example, movements of the hands or facial gestures—witnessing it all day. Still another instruction for self-remembering is: "Wherever one is, whatever one does, remember one's own presence and notice always what one does." These instructions are parallel to those for mindfulness. The similarity between systems is possibly no accident. Both Gurdjieff and Ouspensky traveled in lands in which vipassana or similar techniques were taught precisely to learn such methods, and Gurdjieff was a great borrower, reshaper, and transmitter of Eastern teachings.

In the course of self-remembering, the student realizes (as on the path of insight) that his inner states are in constant flux and that there is no such thing as a permanent "I" within. He sees, instead, an internal cast of characters or "principal features." Each, in turn, dominates the stage and adds its idiosyncrasies to the shape of his personality. With self-observation, the multiplicity of these selves becomes apparent but then falls away. Through observing them, these selves lose their hold as the student ceases to identify with them. As he strengthens his observing I and remains detached from all the others, the student will "wake up." In waking up, he sacrifices his everyday selves. Walker describes this awakened state as "a sense of being present, of being there, of thinking, perceiving, feeling and moving with a certain degree of control and not just automatically." In this state, the witness crystallizes as a constant mental function. The student can see himself with full objectivity.

This order of self-knowledge is preliminary to the highest state, "objective consciousness." In this state, the student sees not only himself but everything else as well with full objectivity. Objective consciousness is the culmination of self-remembering. One's ordinary consciousness is not dislodged, but full objectivity is superimposed on it. This adds an "inner silence" and a liberating sense of distance from the continuing rumblings of the mind. One's experience of the world in objective consciousness is entirely altered; Walker (1969: pp. 47–48) describes this end state in Gurdjieff's training:

> The small limiting "self" of everyday life, the self which insists on its personal rights and separateness, is no longer there to isolate one from everything else, and in its absence one is received into a much wider order of existence . . . as the clamor of thought within dies down into the inner silence, an overwhelming sense of "being" takes its place . . . Such limiting concepts as "yours" or "mine," "his" or "hers" are meaningless . . . and even those old divisions of time into "before" and "after" have been drowned in the fathomless depth of an ever-present "now." So also has disappeared . . . the division between the subject and the object, the knower and the thing known.

Bennett (1973) gives seven levels of man in Gurdjieff's system, the last three of which are "liberated"; these final three are gradations of objective consciousness. As part of his transformation to objective consciousness, one attains liberation from arbitrary, irrational influences from internal and external sources, respectively. The liberated person at the sixth level, for example, is the same as "the bodhisattva of Mahayana Buddhism, or the great saints and *wadis* of Christianity and Islam. He is no longer concerned with his own personal welfare, but has committed himself to the salvation of all creatures."

14. KRISHNAMURTI'S CHOICELESS AWARENESS

J. Krishnamurti, born in South India in the 1890s, was educated in England under the guidance of theosophist Annie Besant. Krishnamurti's view of the human predicament is close to that of Buddhism. The mind and the world, says Krishnamurti, are in everlasting flux: "There is only one fact, impermanence." The human mind clings to a "me" in the face of the insecurity of this flux. But the "me" exists only through identification with what it imagines it has been and wants to be. The "me" is "a mass of contradictions, desires, pursuits, fulfillments and frustrations, with sorrow outweighing joy." One source of sorrow is the constant mental conflict between "what is" and "what should be." The conditioned mind, in Krishnamurti's analysis, flees from the facts of its impermanence, its emptiness, and its sorrow. It builds walls of habit and repetition, and pursues its dreams of the future or clings to that which has been. These defenses paralyze us. They keep us from living in the present moment.

Krishnamurti objects to methods of meditation, the solution so many others advocate. While the mind may try to escape from conditioning through meditation, Krishnamurti says, it simply creates in the very attempt another prison of methods to follow and goals to achieve. He opposes techniques of every kind and urges the putting aside of all authority and tradition: From them, one can only collect more knowledge, while understanding is needed instead. According to Krishnamurti, no technique can free the mind, for any effort by the mind only weaves another net. He, for example, emphatically opposes concentration methods (quoted in Coleman, 1971: p. 114):

> By repeating Amen or *Om* or Coca-Cola indefinitely you obviously have a certain experience because by repetition the mind becomes quiet . . . It is one of the favorite gambits of some teachers of meditation to insist on their pupils learning concentration, that is, fixing the mind on one thought and driving out all other thoughts. This is a most stupid, ugly thing, which any schoolboy can do because he is forced to.

The "meditation" Krishnamurti advocates has no system, least of all "repetition and imitation." He proposes as both means and end a "choiceless awareness," the "experiencing of what is without naming." This state is beyond thought; all thought, he says, belongs to the past, and meditation is always in the present. To be in the present, the mind must relinquish the habits acquired out of the urge to be secure; "its gods and virtues must be given back to the society which bred them." One must let go all thought and all imagining. Advises Krishnamurti (1962: pp. 8–10):

Let the mind be empty, and not filled with the things
of the mind. Then there is only meditation, and not a
meditator who is meditating . . . the mind caught in
imagination can only breed delusions. The mind must
be clear, without movement, and in the light of that
clarity the timeless is revealed.

Krishnamurti seems to advocate an end state only, a meth-
odless method. But on closer scrutiny, he directly tells all
who might hear the "how," while at the same time he insists
that "there is no how; no method." He instructs us "just to
be aware of all this . . . of your own habits, responses." His
means is constantly watching one's own awareness. Krishnamurti's "nontechnique" is more clear from his instructions
to a group of young Indian schoolchildren. He first told
them to sit still with eyes closed and then to watch the
progression of their thoughts. He urged them to continue
this exercise at other times, including when walking or in
bed at night:

You have to watch, as you watch a lizard going by,
walking across the wall, seeing all its four feet, how it
sticks to the wall, you have to watch it, and as you
watch, you see all the movements, the delicacy of its
movements. So in the same way, watch your thinking,
do not correct it, do not suppress it—do not say it is
too hard—just watch it, now, this morning.

He calls this careful attention "self-knowledge." Its essence is "to perceive the ways of your own mind" so that
the mind is "free to be still." When the mind is still, one
understands. The key to understanding is "attention without
the word, the name." He instructs, "Look and be simple":

Where there is attention without reactive thought, reality is.

The process Krishnamurti proposes for self-knowledge duplicates mindfulness training. But Krishnamurti himself would most likely not condone this comparison because of the danger he sees inherent in seeking any goal through a technique. The process he suggests for stilling the mind springs spontaneously from the realization of one's predicament, for to know "that you have been asleep is already an awakened state." This truth, he insists, acts on the mind, setting it free. Krishnamurti (1962: p. 60) assures us:

> When the mind realizes the totality of its own conditioning . . . then all its movements come to an end: It is completely still, without any desire, without any compulsion, without any motive.

This awakening is for Krishnamurti an automatic process. The mind discovers, rather, is caught up in, the solution "through the very intensity of the question itself." This realization cannot be sought: "It comes uninvited." Should one somehow experience the realization of which Krishnamurti speaks, he assures us that a new state would emerge. In this state, one is freed from conditioned habits of perception and cognition, devoid of self. To be in this state, says Krishnamurti, is to love: "Where the self is, love is not." This state brings an "aloneness beyond loneliness" in which there is no movement within the mind, rather a pure experiencing, "attention without motive." One is free from envy, ambition, and the desire for power, and loves with compassion. Here feeling is knowing, in a state of total attention with no watcher. Living in the eternal present, one ceases collecting impressions or experiences; the past dies for one at each moment. With this choiceless awareness, one is free to be simple; as Krishnamurti (Coleman, 1971: p. 95) puts it:

> Be far away, far away from the world of chaos and misery, live in it, untouched . . . The meditative mind is unrelated to the past and to the future and yet is sanely capable of living with clarity and reason.

PART THREE

MEDITATION PATHS: THEIR ESSENTIAL UNITY

In some respects, every method of meditation is like all others, like some others, and like no other. The first level is that of the most general commonalities, disregarding the idiosyncratic variations of technique, emphasis, or belief of any one system. At this most universal level, all meditation systems are variations on a single process for transforming consciousness. The core elements of this process are found in every system, and its specifics undercut ostensible differences among the various schools of meditation.

15. PREPARATION FOR MEDITATION

There is the least common ground among meditation systems on the preparatory groundwork the meditator requires. The systems surveyed here represent the full spectrum of attitudes toward the meditator's need to prepare himself through some kind of purification. They range from the

emphatic insistence on purification as a prelude to meditation voiced in the Bhakti, Kabbalist, Christian, and Sufi
traditions to the views of Gurdjieff and Krishnamurti that
such efforts are pointless if they entail avoiding normal life
situations. Finally, there is the notion among, for example,
TM and Zen schools that genuine purity arises spontaneously as a by-product of meditation itself. Tantrics of the
Bon Marg mark an extreme attitude toward purity in advocating the violation of sexual and other proprieties as part
of spiritual practice.

Ideas about the best setting for meditation likewise cover
a full spectrum. The Desert Fathers withdrew into the Egyptian wilderness to avoid the marketplace and worldly company; hermetic solitude was essential to their program of
severe self-discipline. Modern Indian yogis seek out isolated
mountains and jungle retreats for the same reasons. Western-
ized versions of Indian yoga such as TM, however, oppose
any forced change in the meditator's living habits; instead,
meditation is simply inserted into an otherwise normal daily
agenda. Intensive Zen practice is done ideally in a monastic
setting, but, like TM, it can be part of a meditator's normal
daily round. Both Gurdjieff and Krishnamurti are emphatic
that the settings of family, work, and the marketplace are
the best context for inner discipline, providing the raw
material for meditation.

In most classical meditation systems, however, a monastery or ashram is the optimal environment for meditation,
monks or yogis the ideal companions, the role of the
renunciate the highest calling, and scriptures the best reading. Modern systems such as TM direct the student to or-
ganizational ties and activities while he lives his ordinary
life-style without imposing any major change. Krishnamurti stands alone among spiritual spokesmen in not
advocating that the aspirant seek out the company of oth-

ers on the same path, just as he objects to the aspirant's looking for guidance from a teacher or master—essential elements in every other system.

In propagating no explicit doctrine, Krishnamurti is again unique. Though other schools such as Zen de-emphasize intellectual study, they all have both formal and informal teachings that students assimilate. In some traditions, formal study is a major emphasis: The Benedictine monk, for example, is to spend one-third of his day in study, the other two-thirds in prayer (or meditation) and manual labor.

16. ATTENTION

The strongest agreement among meditation schools is on the importance of retraining attention. All these systems can be broadly categorized in terms of the major strategies for retraining attention described in the Visuddhimagga: concentration or mindfulness. By using the Visuddhimagga map as an example, we can see similarities of technique obscured by the overlay of jargon and ideology.

The differing names used among meditation systems to describe one and the same way and destination are legion. Sometimes the same term is used in special but very different technical senses by various schools. What translates into the English word "void," for example, is used by Indian yogis to refer to jhana states and by Mahayana Buddhists to signify the realization of the essential emptiness of all phenomenon. The former usage denotes a mental state devoid of contents (e.g., the formless jhanas); the latter refers to the voidness of phenomenon. Another example: Phillip Kapleau (1967) distinguishes between zazen and meditation, saying that the two "are not to be confused"; Krishnamurti (1962) says only "choiceless awareness" is really meditation. The recognition that both zazen and choiceless awareness are insight techniques allows one to see that these seemingly unrelated remarks are actually emphasizing the same distinction: that between concentration and insight. By "meditation," Kapleau means concentration, while Krishnamurti denies that concentration practices are within the province of meditation at all.

Table 2 classifies techniques from each meditation system according to the Visuddhimagga typology. The criterion for classification is the mechanics of technique: (a) *concentration,* in which mind focuses on a fixed mental object; (b) *mindfulness,* in which mind observes itself; or (c) both operations present in *integrated* combination.

A second prerequisite for classification is internal consistency in descriptions. If it is a concentration technique, other characteristics of the jhana path are mentioned—for example, increasingly subtle bliss accompanying deepened concentration or loss of sense-consciousness. If it is an insight technique, other characteristics of insight practices, such as the realization of the impersonality of mental processes, must be present. If a combined technique, both concentration techniques as well as insight must be mixed and integrated, as in Theravadan vipassana.

In concentration, the meditator's attentional strategy is to fix his focus on a single percept, constantly bringing back his wandering mind to this object. Some instructions for doing so emphasize an active assertion of the meditator's will to stick with the target percept and resist any wandering. Others suggest a passive mode of simply regenerating the target percept when it is lost in the flow of awareness. Thus, an ancient Theravadan text exhorts the meditator to grit his teeth, clench his fists, and work up a sweat, strug-

TABLE 2
AN APPLIED ATTENTIONAL TYPOLOGY OF
MEDITATION TECHNIQUES

System	Technique	Type
Bhakti	Japa	Concentration
Kabbalah	Kavvanah	Concentration
Hesychasm	Prayer of the Heart	Concentration
Sufi	Zikr	Concentration
Raja Yoga	Samadhi	Concentration
Transcendental Meditation	Transcendental Meditation	Concentration
Kundalini yoga	Siddha yoga	Concentration
Tibetan Buddhism	Vipassana	Integrated
Zen	Zazen	Integrated
Gurdjieff	Self-remembering	Mindfulness
Krishnamurti	Self-knowledge	Mindfulness
Theravada	Vipassana	Integrated

gling to keep his mind fixed on the movements of his respiration; a TM meditator, on the other hand, is told "easily start the mantra" each time he notices his mind has wandered. Though these approaches are opposite on a continuum of activity-passivity, they are equivalent means to constantly reorient to a *single object* of concentration and so develop one-pointedness. With mindfulness techniques— whether Gurdjieff's "self-remembering," Krishnamurti's "self-knowledge," or zazen's "shikan-taza"—the attentional fundamentals are identical: They all entail continuous, full watchfulness of each successive moment, a global vigilance to the meditator's chain of awareness.

There are perhaps few pure types among meditation schools, save for those systems centered around a single technique, for example, TM or Krishnamurti. Most schools are eclectic, using a variety of techniques from both approaches. They make allowances for individual needs, tailoring techniques to the student's progress. Sufis, for example, mainly use the zikr, a concentration practice, but also at times employ insight techniques like *Muragaba,* which is attention to the flow of one's own awareness. For simplicity, in the preceding sections a specific technique has been emphasized, generally the main one.

Different meditation systems may espouse wholly contradictory views from one another on the necessity for virtually every preparatory act, be it a specific environment, the need for a teacher, or prior knowledge of what to expect from meditation. But the need for the meditator to retrain his attention, whether through concentration or mindfulness, is the single invariant ingredient in the recipe for altering consciousness of every meditation system.

17. SEEING WHAT
YOU BELIEVE

The meditator's beliefs determine how he interprets and labels his meditation experiences. When a Sufi enters a state in which he is no longer aware of his senses, and his only thought is that of Allah, he knows this to be fana; when a yogi is no longer aware of his senses, and his mind is totally focused on his deity, then he will say he has entered samadhi. Many different names are used to describe one and the same experience: jhana, samyana or samadhi, fana, Daat, turiya, the great fixation, and transcendental consciousness. All seem to refer to a single state with identical characteristics. These many terms for a single state come from Theravadan Buddhism, raja yoga, Sufism, Kabbalah, kundalini yoga, Zen, and TM, respectively.

The history of religion is rife with instances of a transcendental experience interpreted in terms of assumptions specific to time, place, and belief. The Indian saint Ramana Maharshi saw his own transcendental states in terms of Advait philosophy. He conjectures that during Saul's great experience on the Damascus road, when he returned to normal consciousness, he interpreted what happened in terms of Christ and the Christians because at the time he was preoccupied with them (Chadwick, 1966). A person's reference group gives him a gloss on his inner realities; Berger and Luckmann (1967) point out that while "Saul may have become Paul in the aloneness of religious ecstasy . . . he could *remain* Paul only in the context of the Christian community that recognized him as such and confirmed the 'new being' in which he now located this identity."

The interaction among the meditator's beliefs, his internal state, and his self-definition is made clear by a recent example drawn from kundalini yoga. In this tradition, the guru is crucial to the meditator both in helping him achieve sought-after meditation states and in interpreting and confirming the significance of these same experiences.

Swami Rudrananda, a teacher of kundalini yoga, describes the incident that preceded his being awarded the rank of swami. While he was meditating, his master touched him on the shoulder, at which point (Rudi, 1973: p. 85):

> I immediately felt within me a surge of great spiritual force which hurled me against the stone walls and allowed a great electric shock to send a spasm of contortions through my body. Movements similar to those

of an epileptic controlled my body for about an hour. Many strange visions appeared and I felt things opening within me that had never been opened before.

Rudrananda took his experience to confirm his worthiness of the title "swami," an advanced status. While a set of beliefs about altered states in meditation may render them safe, the meditator does not need specific foreknowledge of these states to experience them. In his autobiography (1972), for example, Swami Muktananda tells how his guru would assign him a meditation practice but give no further hints as to what to expect beyond the barest instructions. When Muktananda subsequently entered extraordinary states, he did so naively. Only after undergoing these states did he chance upon books that gave him an interpretive framework for understanding what had happened. Sri Aurobindo's biographer, Satprem (1970: p. 256), likewise describes the unusual states Aurobindo experienced in the course of his spiritual development but notes:

Sri Aurobindo was the first to be baffled by his own experience and . . . it took him some years to understand exactly what had happened. We have described the . . . experience . . . as though the stages had been linked very carefully, each with its explanatory label, but the explanations came long afterwards, at that moment he had no guiding landmarks.

18. ALTERED STATES IN MEDITATION

In meditation, method is the seed of the goal: The contours of the state the meditator reaches depend on how he arrived. The concentrative path leads the meditator to merge with his meditation object in jhana and then to transcend it. As he reaches deeper levels, the bliss becomes more compelling, yet more subtle. In the way of mindfulness, the meditator's mind witnesses its own workings, and he comes to perceive increasingly finer segments of his stream of thought. As his perception sharpens, he becomes increasingly detached from what he witnesses, finally turning away from all awareness in the nirvanic state. In this state, there is no experience whatever.

Every system that uses concentration describes the same journey into jhana, though different schools cast the descriptions in differing terms. The key attributes of this state are always the same: loss of sense awareness, one-pointed attention to one object to the exclusion of all other thoughts, and sublimely rapturous feelings. Systems that use mindfulness describe the path of insight: increasingly finer perception of the meditator's mind, detachment from these events, and a compelling focus on the present moment. The nirvanic state, per se, is not necessarily cited as the end point of this progression.

These two altered states are the prototypical altered states in meditation. They do not, however, exhaust all the possible changes in consciousness that meditation brings. Attention is extremely flexible and can change awareness in many more ways than the two major ones described here. Attentional retraining can also be linked with exercises in other biosystems, for example, with movement in Sufi dancing. Additional practices such as controlled respiration, fasting, visualizations, or adopting strong beliefs all contribute to the final shape of the altered state, over and above the effects of the meditator's attentional exercises.

Attention is the key to meditative altered states, but the addition of other practices compounds the complexity of the calculus of the resulting changes in awareness. One example of a more complex altered state is that produced by the kundalini yoga technique of shaktipatdiksha, the direct transmission of a meditative altered state from teacher to student through look or touch. The seizure-like activity in this state may be due to breath-control exercises as well as to expectations arising from the intense guru-student relationship, and perhaps in part to modeling—all in addition to the basic effects of concentration. The more means used to alter consciousness, the more intricate the topography of the resulting state.

The literature of every meditation system describes an altered state. Jhana is the prototype of one variety, in which the altered state is a neatly delimited enclave of awareness set off from other states. Jhanic states are mutually exclusive of the normal major states: waking, sleeping, and dreaming. Another type of altered state, however, merges with these major states. This merger appends new functions on the normal states, changing their character. This meets Tart's (1971) criterion for "higher states of consciousness": (1) all functions of "lower" states are available, that is, waking, sleeping, and dreaming; and (2) some new aspects, derivative of an altered state, are present in addition. This kind of transmutation of awareness is an altered *trait* of consciousness, an enduring change transforming the meditator's every moment. The "awakened" state is the ideal type of an altered trait of consciousness. Virtually every system of meditation recognizes the awakened state as the ultimate goal of meditation (Table 3).

In TM, for example, "transcendental consciousness" is the altered state that infuses normal states. The stages ensuing after "transcendental consciousness" from further evolution are "cosmic consciousness," "God consciousness," and finally, "unity." Each represents a deeper infusion of meditative awareness into normal states. Most systems agree that such altered traits occur gradually and to differing degrees. In the Visuddhimagga, for example, there is a similar gradient in the four levels of purification arising from increasingly deep penetration of the nirvanic state.

The goal of all meditation paths, whatever their ideology, source, or methods, is to transform the meditator's consciousness. In the process, the meditator dies to his past self and is reborn to a new level of experience. Whether through concentration in jhana or through insight in nirvana, the altered states the meditator gains are dramatic in their discontinuity with his normal states. But the ultimate transformation for the meditator is a newer state still: the awakened state, which mixes with and re-creates his normal consciousness.

Each path labels this end state differently. But no matter how diverse the names, these paths all propose the same basic formula in an alchemy of the self: the diffusion of the effects of meditation into the meditator's waking, dreaming, and sleep states. At the outset, this diffusion requires the meditator's effort. As he progresses, it becomes easier for him to maintain prolonged meditative awareness in the midst of his other activities. As the states produced by his meditation meld with his waking activity, the awakened state ripens. When it reaches full maturity, it lastingly changes his consciousness, transforming his experience of himself and of his universe.

TABLE 3
NAMES FOR THE AWAKENED STATE

System	Name of Awakened State
Bhakti	Sahaj samadhi
Kabbalah	Devekut
Hesychasm	Purity of heart
Sufi	Baqa
Raja Yoga	Sahaj samadhi; jivamukti
Transcendental Meditation	Cosmic consciousness; God-consciousness; unity
Kundalini Yoga	Turiyatita; Siddha
Tibetan Buddhism	Boddhisattva
Zen	Mujodo no taigeu ("no-mind")
Gurdjieff	Objective consciousness
Krishnamurti	Choiceless awareness
Theravadan Buddhism	Arahantship

Though sources like the Visuddhimagga draw distinctions according to the angle of entrance to this transformation (concentration or insight), it is likely that at this point all paths merge. Or, more to the point, from our perspective the similarities may far outweigh the differences. An awakened being transcends his own origins; persons of any faith can recognize him as exceptional or "perfect," or—if so inclined—revere him as a saint.

PART FOUR

THE PSYCHOLOGY
OF MEDITATION

The meditation systems of the East are applications of spiritual psychologies. As such, they have great potential for cross-fertilization with Western psychology—a potential just beginning to be explored.

19. ABHIDHAMMA:
AN EASTERN PSYCHOLOGY

Attempts to forge a systematic understanding of human personality and mental health did not originate with contemporary Western psychology. Our formal psychology, about a hundred years old, is merely a recent version of an endeavor probably as old as civilization. Western models of health and normality are the product of European and American culture, and are only one set of the innumerable ideals and norms that people in many times and places have articulated.

Some of the richest alternative sources of well-formulated

psychologies and visions of human possibilities are Eastern religions. Quite separate from the vagaries of cosmology and the dogma of beliefs, most major Asian religions have at their core a psychology little known to the masses of adherents to the faith but quite familiar to the appropriate "professionals," be they yogis, monks, or priests. This is the practical psychology that people apply to discipline their own minds and hearts in order to attain a more ideal state of being.

Just as there is a multitude of personality theories in Western civilization, there are numerous Eastern psychologies. But while there are major differences of belief and worldview among the religions that contain the Eastern psychologies, there is far less difference among the psychologies themselves. One common feature of these psychologies is that they find fault with human beings as they are, positing an ideal mode of being that anyone who seeks with diligence can attain. The path to this transformation is always via a far-reaching change, so that these ideal qualities may become stable traits. The Eastern psychologies also agree that the main means to this transformation of self is meditation.

One of the most systematic and intricately laid out of these psychologies is that of classical Buddhism. Called in the Pali language of Buddha's day *Abhidhamma* (or *Abhidharma* in Sanskrit), which means "the ultimate doctrine," this psychology elaborates Gautama Buddha's original insights into human nature. Since it stems from Buddha's basic teachings, *Abhidhamma,* or a psychology very much like it, is at the core of all the various branches of Buddhism. From its fullest development during the first millennium after Buddha's death, it has been preserved largely unchanged by the Theravadan Buddhists as part of their scriptures, the Pali Canon.

Although Abhidhamma was developed in India fifteen or

more centuries ago, present-day Buddhists continue to apply it in various forms as a guide to the workings of the mind. The insights of Gautama Buddha in the fifth century B.C.— and the psychology that springs from these insights—have been refined and evolved into the various lineages, teachings, and schools of Buddhism, in a process of evolution akin to that by which, for example, Freud's thought developed into disparate schools of psychoanalysis.*

Many Abhidhamma principles represent the psychological teachings common to all Eastern faiths rather than those limited to Buddhism. As a prototype of Asian psychology, Abhidhamma presents us with a set of concepts for understanding mental activity and an ideal for mental health that differ markedly from the concepts of Western psychology. Like other Eastern psychologies, Abhidhamma contains an ideal of the perfected personality around which its analysis of the workings of the mind is oriented. As Nyanaponika Thera, a modern Buddhist scholar-monk put it, "In the Buddhist doctrine, mind is the starting point, the focal point, and also, as the liberated and purified mind of the Saint, the culminating point" (1962, p. 12).

Personality in Buddhist Psychology

An ancient tale is emblematic of Abhidhamma's extremely analytic attitude toward the person. A beautiful young woman had quarreled with her husband and was running away back home to her family. She passed by a monk, who, as he walked on his daily round for alms, saw the woman

*An excellent description of Abhidhamma is in Lama Govinda's *The Psychological Attitude of Early Buddhist Philosophy* (1969). For more detailed reviews of Abhidhamma see also Guenther (1976), Narada (1968), and Nyanaponika (1971).

pass by him "dressed up like a celestial nymph." The monk, who at the time was reflecting on the nature of the human skeleton, looked up and noticed the whiteness of her teeth. A little later, her husband came by, in hot pursuit. He asked, "Venerable sir, did you by any chance see a woman?" Replied the monk (Buddhaghosa, 1976: p. 22):

> Whether it was a man or woman
> That went by I noticed not;
> But only that on this high road
> There goes a bag of bones.

Since the old monk in the story was meditating on one of 32 parts of the body—the skeleton—for him that aspect of the pretty woman loomed largest. Through keen observation in meditation the monk was able to become so detached from all the constituents of body and mind that no one of them held any greater value than any other. From this perspective a person's bones are as noteworthy as his or her thoughts. This degree of utter detachment reflects the spirit of Abhidhamma as it surveys and dissects the human personality.

What we denote by the word "personality" equates most closely in Abhidhamma to a concept of *atta,* or self. But a central premise of Abhidhamma is that there is no abiding self whatsoever, only an impersonal aggregate of processes that come and go. The semblance of personality springs from the intermingling of these impersonal processes. What appears to be "self" is the sum total of body parts, thoughts, sensations, desires, memories, and so on. The only continuous thread in the mind is *bhava,* the continuity of consciousness over time. Each successive moment of our awareness is shaped by the previous moment, and will in turn determine the following moment. It is bhava that connects one mo-

ment of consciousness to that which follows. We may identify the "self" with psychological activities such as our
thoughts, memories, or perceptions, yet all these phenomena
are part of a continued flow. The human personality, says
Abhidhamma, is like a river that keeps a constant form,
seemingly a single identity, though not a single drop is the
same as a moment ago. In this view "there is no actor apart
from action, no percipient apart from perception, no con-
scious subject behind consciousness" (Van Aung, 1972: p. 7).
In the words of Buddha (Samyutta-Nikaya, 1972, I: p. 35):

> Just as when the parts are set together
> There arises the word "chariot,"
> So does the notion of a being
> When the aggregates are present.

The study of personality in Buddhism does not deal with
a complex of postulated entities, such as "ego" or "unconscious," but with a series of events. The basic event is the
ongoing relationship of mental states to sense objects—for
example, a feeling of desire (the mental state) toward a
beautiful woman (the sense object). A person's mental states
are in constant flux from moment to moment; their rate of
change is reckoned in microseconds. The basic method Abhidhamma offers for studying the mind's multitudinous
changes is introspection, a close and systematic observation
of one's own experience.

Without careful introspection one might think that a state
such as desire can persist without interruption for a long
while, but Abhidhamma says this is not so. For example,
even if one is in the throes of passionate lovemaking, where
desire seems overwhelming, Abhidhamma has it that if one
were to closely monitor each successive mental state, one
would see that that desire is actually interspersed with innu-

merable other feelings that come and go. Not only do a person's mental states vary from moment to moment; so also do sense objects. While a person might think that during lovemaking she pays attention only to her lover, close scrutiny of her stream of consciousness would reveal that, in addition, a multitude of other objects occupy her mind and senses. These might include a variety of pleasant sensations, various sounds from near and far, and an assortment of smells, tastes, and sights. Random memories, future plans, and other thoughts would mingle with these objects of the senses.

Mental Factors

In Abhidhamma, in addition to the objects of the five senses, there are thoughts; that is, the thinking mind itself is counted as the "sixth" sense. Thus, just as a sound or sight can be the object of a mental state, so can a thought—for example, the thought "I should take out the garbage" might be the object of a mental state of aversion. Each mental state is composed of a set of properties, called mental factors, that combine to flavor and define that state.

The Abhidhamma system discussed here enumerates 53 categories of such mental factors; in other branches of Buddhism the count varies up to 175. In any one mental state only a sub-set of the factors are present. The unique qualities of each mental state are determined by which factors it combines. The moment of dislike for taking out the garbage, for example, would have a more complex combination than simple aversion; a dozen or more other mental factors, such as misperception of what taking out the garbage is really like, would combine with aversion.

Mental states come and go in a lawful and orderly manner. As in Western psychology, Abhidhamma theorists believe each mental state derives in part from biological and situational influences, in addition to a carryover from the preceding psychological moment. Each state in turn determines the particular combination of factors in the next mental state.

Mental factors are the key to what we in the West know as "karma," or in Pali, *kamma*. In Abhidhamma *kamma* is a technical word for the principle that every deed is motivated by underlying mental states. In Abhidhamma, as in many Eastern psychologies, a given behavior is in essence ethically neutral. Its moral nature cannot be determined without taking into account the underlying motives of the person as he or she performed it. The acts of someone who has a negative mix of mental factors—who acts, for example, from malice or greed—are evil, even though the act itself might seem to an observer neither good nor bad. The *Dhammapada,* a collection of verses spoken by Gautama Buddha, begins with a statement of the Abhidhamma doctrine of karma (Babbitt, 1965, p. 3):

All that we are is the result of what we have thought: it is founded on our thoughts, it is made up of our thoughts. If a man speaks or acts with an evil thought, pain follows him, as the wheel follows the foot of the ox that draws the wagon. . . . If a man speaks or acts with a pure thought, happiness follows him, like a shadow that never leaves him.

The Abhidhamma distinguishes between mental factors that are *kusula*—pure, wholesome, or healthy—and *akusula*—impure, unwholesome, or unhealthy. Most perceptual, cognitive, and affective mental factors fit into either the healthy or unhealthy category. The judgment of "healthy" or "unhealthy" was arrived at empirically, on the basis of the collective experience of large numbers of early Buddhist meditators. Their criterion was whether a particular mental factor facilitated or interfered with their attempts to still their minds in meditation. Those factors that interfered with meditation were designated as "unhealthy," those that aided as "healthy."

In addition to healthy or unhealthy factors, there are seven neutral properties present in every mental state. Apperception *(phassa)* is the mere awareness of an object; perception *(sanna)*, its first recognition as belonging to one or the other of the senses; volition *(cetana)*, the conditioned reaction that accompanies the first perception of an object; feeling *(vedana)*, the sensations aroused by the object; one-pointedness *(ekaggata)*, the focusing of awareness; spontaneous attention *(manasikara)*, the involuntary directing of attention due to attraction by the object; and psychic energy *(jivitindriya)*, which lends vitality to and unites the other six factors. These factors provide a basic framework of consciousness in which the healthy and unhealthy factors are embedded. The particular combination of factors that embeds in this framework varies from moment to moment.

Unhealthy Mental Factors. The central unhealthy factor, delusion, is perceptual: delusion *(moha)* is defined as a cloudiness of mind that leads to misperception of the object of awareness. Delusion is seen in Abhidhamma as basic ignorance, the primary root of human suffering. This misperception of the true nature of things—the simple failure to see clearly, without bias or prejudice of any kind—is the core of all unhealthy mental states. Delusion, for example, leads to "false view" or misdiscernment *(ditthi)*. False view entails placing something in the wrong category or miscategorization. The working of these factors is clear in the case of the

paranoid, who misperceives as threatening someone who
wishes him or her no harm, and so categorizes the other
person as part of a fancied conspiracy against him or herself.
The Buddha is quoted as saying that while a person's mind
is dominated by false view, whatever he might do or aspire
to could only "lead him to an undesirable, unpleasant, and
disagreeable state, to woe and suffering" (*Anguttara nikaya,*
1975, I, p. 23). Among the pernicious false views the Buddha
explicitly criticized is one of the pervasive assumptions of
many Western personality theories, namely, that there is a
fixed "self" or "ego." In Abhidhamma there is no self as
such but a "self-consuming process of physical and mental
phenomena which continually arise and again disappear immediately" (Nyanatiloka, 1972, p. 25).

Perplexity *(vicikiccha)* denotes the inability to decide or
make a correct judgment. When this factor dominates a
person's mind he or she is filled with doubt and, at the
extreme, can become paralyzed. Other unhealthy cognitive
factors are shamelessness *(ahirika)* and remorselessness *(anot-
tappa)*; these attitudes allow a person to disregard the opin-
ions of others and one's own internalized standards. When
these factors hold sway, a person views evil acts without
compunction, and so is apt to misbehave. Indeed, these
factors are prerequisites for the mental states that underlie
any act of ill-will. Another unwholesome factor that might
lead to wrongdoing is egoism *(mana)*. This attitude of self-
interest causes people to view objects solely in terms of
fulfilling their own desires or needs. The concatenation of
these three mental factors in a single moment—shamelessness, remorselessness, and selfishness—is undoubtedly often
the basis for much human evil.

The rest of the unhealthy mental factors are affective.
Agitation *(uddhacca)* and worry *(kukkucca)* are states of distractedness, remorse, and rumination. These factors create a

state of anxiety, the central feature of most mental disorder. Another set of unhealthy factors relate to clinging: greed *(lobha)*, avarice *(macchariya)*, and envy *(issa)* denote different kinds of grasping attachment to an object, while aversion *(dosa)* is the negative side of attachment. Greed and aversion are found in all negative mental states, and always combine with delusion. Two final unhealthy factors are contraction *(thina)* and torpor *(middha)*. These factors lend a rigid inflexibility to mental states. When these negative factors predominate, a person's mind as well as body is prone to sluggishness.

Healthy Mental Factors. Each of the unhealthy factors is opposed by a healthy factor. These factors are either healthy or unhealthy; there is no middle ground. The means in Abhidhamma for attaining a healthy mental state is to replace the unhealthy factors with their polar opposites. The principle that allows this is akin to "reciprocal inhibition" as used in systematic desensitization, where relaxation inhibits its physiologic opposite, tension. For each negative mental factor there is a corresponding positive factor that overrides it. When a given healthy factor is present in a mental state, the unhealthy factor it suppresses cannot arise.

The central healthy factor is insight *(panna)*, the opposite of delusion. Insight, in the sense of "clear perception of the object as it really is," suppresses delusion, the fundamental unhealthy factor. These two factors cannot co-exist in a single mental state: where there is clarity, there cannot be delusion; nor where there is delusion in any degree can there be clarity. Mindfulness *(sati)* is the continued clear comprehension of an object; this essential partner of insight steadies and holds clarity in a person's mind. Insight and mindfulness are the primary healthy factors; when they are present in a mental state, the other healthy factors tend to be present also.

The presence of these two healthy factors is sufficient to suppress all the unhealthy factors.

Some healthy factors require certain circumstances to arise. The twin cognitive factors of modesty *(hiri)*, which inhibits shamelessness, and discretion *(ottappa)*, the opposite of remorselessness, come to mind only when there is a thought of an evil act. Modesty and discretion are always connected with rectitude *(cittujjukata)*, the attitude of correct judgment. Another healthy factor is confidence *(saddha)*, a sureness based on correct perception. This group of mental factors—modesty, discretion, rectitude, and confidence— act together to produce virtuous behavior as judged both by personal and social standards.

The cluster of unhealthy factors formed by greed, avarice, envy, and aversion are opposed by the healthy factors of nonattachment *(alobha)*, nonaversion *(adosa)*, impartiality *(tatramajjhata)*, and composure *(passadhi)*, which reflect the physical and mental tranquility that arises from diminishing feelings of attachment. The above four factors replace a grasping or rejecting attitude with an even-mindedness to- ward whatever object might arise in a person's awareness.

The unhealthy factors of greed, egoism, envy, and aversion, for example, might cause a person to crave a more prestigious job with higher pay and glamor, or to envy someone who had such a job, or to despise his or her own lesser position. The opposing healthy factors of composure, nonattachment, nonaversion, and impartiality, on the other hand, would lead the person to weigh the advantages of pay and prestige against such drawbacks as more pressure and stress, to assess fairly the strengths that have led another to have such a job and the weaknesses that make the person perform less well than he or she should. Finally, these four healthy factors would let one weigh whatever advantages one's own job might have, in what respects it might be unsuitable, what one's genuine capabilities are, and how to use them to get a better position within the limits of one's skills. Even more important, impartiality would lead one to regard the whole situation coolly, neither unhappy that one does not have a better job, nor despising one's own, nor resigned to accepting with despair an unsuitable job. These four healthy mental factors allow one to accept things as they are, but also to make whatever changes seem appropriate.

Body and mind are seen as interconnected in Abhidhamma. While every factor affects both body and mind, the final set of healthy factors are the only ones explicitly described as having both physical and psychological effects. These are buoyancy *(ahuta)*, pliancy *(muduta)*, adaptability *(kammannata)*, and proficiency *(pagunnata)*. When these factors arise a person thinks and acts with a natural looseness and ease, performing at the peak of his or her skills. They suppress the unhealthy factors of contraction and torpor, which dominate the mind in such states as depression. These healthy factors make one able to adapt physically and mentally to changing conditions, meeting whatever challenges may arise.

Table 4 lists the healthy and unhealthy factors. In the Abhidhamma psychodynamic, healthy and unhealthy mental factors are mutually inhibiting; the presence of one suppresses its opposite. But there is not always a one-to-one correspondence between a pair of healthy and unhealthy factors; in some cases a single healthy factor will inhibit a set of unhealthy factors—nonattachment alone, for example, inhibits greed, avarice, envy, and aversion. Certain key factors will inhibit the entire opposite set; for example, when delusion is present, not a single positive factor can arise along with it.

It is a person's *kamma* that determines whether he or she

TABLE 4
HEALTHY AND UNHEALTHY
MENTAL FACTORS

Unhealthy Factors	*Healthy Factors*
Perceptual/Cognitive:	
Delusion	Insight
False View	Mindfulness
Shamelessness	Modesty
Recklessness	Discretion
Egoism	Confidence
Affective:	
Agitation	Composure
Greed	Nonattachment
Aversion	Nonaversion
Envy	Impartiality
Avarice	Buoyancy
Worry	Pliancy
Contraction	Adaptability
Torpor	Proficiency
Perplexity	Rectitude

will experience predominantly healthy or unhealthy states. The particular combination of factors are the outcome of biological and situational influences as well as the carryover from one's previous states of mind. The factors usually arise as a group, either positive or negative. In any given mental state the factors composing it arise in differing strengths; whichever factor is the strongest determines how a person experiences and acts at any given moment.

Although all the negative factors may be present, the state experienced will be quite different depending on whether, for example, it is greed or torpor that dominates the mind. The hierarchy of strength of the factors, then, determines whether a specific state will be negative or positive. When a particular factor or set of factors occurs frequently in a person's mental states, then it becomes a personality trait. The sum total of a person's habitual mental factors determines their personality type.

Personality Types

The Abhidhamma model for personality types follows directly from the principle that mental factors arise in differing strengths. If a person's mind is habitually dominated by a particular factor or set of factors, these will determine personality, motives, and behavior. The uniqueness of each person's pattern of mental factors gives rise to individual differences in personality over and above the broad categories of the main types. The person in whom delusion predominates is one of the common types, as are the hateful person, in whom aversion predominates, and the lustful person, in whom greed is strong. A more positive type is the intelligent person, in whom mindfulness and insight are strong.

The Abhidhamma view of human motivation stems from its analysis of mental factors and their influence on behavior. It is a person's mental states that move the person to seek one thing and avoid another. His or her mental states guide every act. If the mind is dominated by greed, then this will become the predominant motive, and one will behave accordingly, seeking to gain the object of one's greed. If egoism is a powerful factor, then the person will act in a self-aggrandizing manner. Each personality type is, in this sense, a motivational type also.

The Visuddhimagga devotes a section to recognizing the main personality types, since each kind of person must be treated in a way that suits his or her disposition. One method it recommends for evaluating personality type is careful observation of how a person stands and moves. The lustful or sensual person, for example, is said to be graceful in gait; the hateful person drags the feet as he or she walks; the deluded person paces quickly. A typical rule of thumb for this analysis goes (Vajiranana, 1962, p. 99):

Of the lustful the footprint is divided in the middle,
Of unfriendly man it leaves a trail behind.
The print of the deluded one is an impression quickly
    made . . .

It goes on to note that a Buddha leaves a perfectly even footprint, since his mind is calm and his body poised.

The author of the Visuddhimagga recognized that every detail of life is a clue to character; this fifth-century manual gives a remarkably complete behavioral profile for each personality type. The sensual person, it tells us, is charming, polite, and replies courteously when addressed. When such persons sleep, they make their beds carefully, lie down gently, and move little while asleep. They perform their duties artistically; sweep with smooth and even strokes, and do a thorough job. In general they are skillful, polished, tidy, and circumspect workers. They dress neatly and tastefully. When they eat they prefer soft, sweet food that is well cooked and served in sumptuous fashion; they eat slowly, take small bites, and relish the taste. On seeing any pleasing object they stop to admire it, and are attracted by its merits, but do not notice its faults. They leave such an object with regret. But on the negative side they are often pretentious, deceitful, vain, covetous, dissatisfied, lascivious, and frivolous.

The hateful person, by contrast, stands stiffly. These persons make their bed carelessly and in haste, sleep with their bodies tense, and reply in anger when awakened. When they work they are rough and careless; when they sweep the broom makes a harsh, scraping noise. Their clothes are likely to be too tight and unfinished. When they eat their preference is for pungent food that tastes sharp and sour; they eat hurriedly without noticing the taste, though they dislike food with a mild taste. They are uninterested in objects of beauty, and notice even the slightest fault while overlooking merits. They are often angry, full of malice, ungrateful, envious, and mean.

The third type is distinct from these two. The deluded person stands in a slovenly manner. Their beds are untidy, they sleep in a sprawl, and arise sluggishly, grunting with complaints. As workers they are unskillful and messy; they sweep awkwardly and at random, leaving bits of rubbish behind. Their clothes are loose and untidy. They do not care what they eat, and will eat whatever comes their way; they are sloppy eaters, putting large lumps of food in the mouth and smearing the face with food. They have no idea whether an object is beautiful or not, but believe whatever others tell them, and so praise or disapprove accordingly. They often show sloth and torpor, are easily distracted, are given to remorse and perplexity, but can also be obstinate and tenacious.

The Visuddhimagga goes on to specify the optimal conditions that should be arranged for persons of each type when they begin to meditate. The first goal in their training is to counteract their dominant psychological tendencies, and so bring their mind into balance. For this reason the conditions prescribed for each type are not those they would naturally choose. The cottage given to the sensual person, for example, is an unwashed grass hut that ought to be "spattered with dirt, full of bats, dilapidated, too high or too low, in bleak surroundings, threatened by lions and tigers, with a muddy, uneven path, where even the bed and chair are full of bugs. And it should be ugly and unsightly, exciting loathing as soon as looked at" (p. 109). The Visuddhimagga details the other conditions that suit the sensual person (Buddhaghosa, 1976, pp. 109–110):

Suitable garments have torn-off edges with threads hanging down, harsh to the touch like hemp, soiled, heavy and hard to wear. And the right kind of bowl for him is an ugly clay bowl or a heavy and misshappen iron bowl as unappetising as a skull. The right kind of road for him on which to wander for alms is disagreeable, with no village near, and uneven. The right kind of village for him is where people wander about as if oblivious of him. Suitable people to serve him are unsightly, ill-favoured, with dirty clothes, ill-smelling and disgusting, who serve him his gruel and rice as if they were throwing it rudely at him. The right kind of food is made of broken rice, stale buttermilk, sour gruel, curry of old vegetables, or anything at all that is merely for filling the stomach.

The suitable conditions for the hateful person, on the other hand, are as pleasant, comfortable, and easy as can be arranged. For the deluded person, things are to be made simple and clear, and quite as pleasant and comfortable as for the hateful person. In each case the environment is tailored to inhibit the kind of mental factor that usually dominates each personality type: the lustful person finds little to be greedy about, the hateful person little to despise, and for the deluded person things are clear. This program of environments designed to promote mental health is an ancient predecessor to what modern advocates of similar plans call "milieu therapy." The Buddha also saw that different types of people would take more readily to different kinds of meditation, and so he devised a wide variety of meditation methods tailored to fit different personality types.

Mental Health

The factors that form one's mental states from moment to moment determine one's mental health. The operational definition of mental disorder in Abhidhamma is simple: the absence of healthy factors, and presence of unhealthy factors. Each variety of mental disorder stems from the hold of certain unhealthy factors on the mind. The special character of each unhealthy factor leads to a particular disorder—egoism, for example, underlies the purely self-interested actions that we in Western psychology call "sociopathic" behavior; agitation and worry are the anxiety at the core of neuroses; aversion tied to a specific object or situation is a phobia.

The criterion for mental health is equally simple: the presence of the healthy factors, and absence of unhealthy factors, in a person's psychological economy. The healthy factors, besides supplanting unhealthy ones, also provide a necessary mental environment for a group of positive affective states that cannot arise in the presence of the unhealthy factors. These include loving-kindness *(karuna)* and "altruistic joy" *(mudita)*—that is, taking pleasure in the happiness of others.

The normal person has a mixture of healthy and unhealthy factors in the flow of mental states. Each of us at times experiences periods of wholly healthy or unhealthy mental states as our stream of consciousness flows on. Very few people, however, experience only healthy mental states, and thus all of us are "unhealthy" in this sense. Indeed, one scripture quotes the Buddha as saying of normal people: "All worldlings are deranged." The goal of psychological development in Abhidhamma is to increase the amount of healthy states—and correspondingly, decrease unhealthy ones—in a person's mind. At the peak of mental health, no unhealthy factors arise at all in a person's mind. Although this is the ideal that each person is urged to seek, it is, of course, rarely realized.

One reason few people achieve ideal mental health is due to *anusayas,* latent tendencies of the mind toward unhealthy mental states. Anusayas lie dormant in the person's mind until an opportune moment arises for them to surface. Seven of the unhealthy factors are particularly strong anusayas: greed, false view, delusion, aversion, doubt, pride, and agitation. While a person experiences a healthy mental state, these anusayas are in abeyance, but they are never far from taking over when the moment is ripe. The final criterion for full mental health is to have eradicated the anusayas from one's mind, thereby eliminating even the tendency toward unhealthy states of mind. The principle of anusayas is the closest approximation in Abhidhamma to the Western concept of the unconscious.

As a catalogue of the mental properties we experience from moment to moment, the Abhidhamma list of mental factors is by no means exhaustive. The possibilities for categorizing mental states are countless; the Abhidhamma theorists do not pretend to offer a total compendium. But theirs is a purposeful analysis; their categories are designed to help a person recognize, and so control, key states of mind so that he or she may ultimately be rid of unhealthy states. The practicing Buddhist embarks on a coordinated program of environmental, behavioral, and attentional control to attain his or her final goal, a plateau of purely healthy mental states. In the classical Buddhist path a person who sought this plateau of health would enter the controlled surroundings of a monastery, regulate his or her actions by taking the vows of a monk or nun, and, most important, meditate.

Meditation: The Path to Mental Health. Once people have become familiar with the categories of healthy and unhealthy mental factors so that they can see them at play in their own minds, they will find that simply knowing a state is unhealthy does little or nothing to end it. For example, if a person resents the predominance of unhealthy factors in the mind, or if he wishes they would go away, he is merely adding aversion and desire to the psychological mix. The strategy the Abhidhamma offers for attaining healthy states is neither directly to seek them nor to be averse to unhealthy states. The recommended approach is meditation.

In Abhidhamma, attaining a healthy mental state means replacing the unhealthy factors with their polar opposites. The principle that allows this is akin to "reciprocal inhibition" as used in systematic desensitization, where relaxation inhibits its physiologic opposite, tension. For each negative mental facet there is a corresponding positive factor which overrides it. When a given healthy factor is present in a mental state, the unhealthy factor it suppresses cannot arise.

In the Abhidhamma psychodynamic, positive and negative mental factors are mutually inhibiting; the presence of one suppresses its opposite. But there is not always a one-to-one correspondence between a pair of healthy and unhealthy factors; in some cases a single healthy factor will inhibit a set of unhealthy factors—non-attachment alone, for example, inhibits greed, avarice, envy, and aversion. Certain key factors will inhibit the entire opposite set; for example, when delusion is present, not a single positive factor can arise with it.

For each unwholesome factor there exists at least one wholesome factor that effectively blocks the entry of its negative counterpart into consciousness. In cases where specific unwholesome factors are particularly intense, their opposites must be repeatedly invoked in order to eradicate them. As the influence of the unhealthy factors dwindles, the strength of the corresponding healthy influences increases. Progress in meditation may be described solely as the cultivation of wholesome qualities at the expense of unwholesome ones, a process aiming at the eradication of all unwholesome factors from one's mind.

The dynamics of the wholesome-unwholesome duality clear the way for a mind cleansed of unwholesome factors. Abhidhamma posits that wholesome factors cannot exist in the same mind moment as unwholesome factors, because of specific antagonistic relationships between mental factors. The mind cannot be felt to be both heavy and light, both clear and hazy, at the same time. The existence of one at a given moment nullifies the other. Normal waking consciousness involves an oscillation between the two influences, but a complete absence of all of the unhealthy factors for any great length of time is rarely found in normal awareness.

Abhidhamma spells out two distinct methods of reorganization of consciousness designed to lessen and finally eradicate the impact of the unwholesome factors. The first employs a meditative strategy of concentration; the second, one of mindfulness. Progress in one or the other form of meditation may be understood and explained solely in terms of the restructuring of roles played by various mental factors.

The Abhidhamma assumes as a starting point a person whose mind is bound by unwholesome factors. When the wholesome factors are weak, a person's psychological health is poor; as seen through the Abhidhamma lens, the mental state of a normal person is rather dour (Nyanaponika, 1949, p. 67):

A general heaviness and unwieldiness of the mental processes results: force of habit predominates; changes and adaptations are undertaken slowly and unwillingly, and to the smallest possible degree; thought is rigid, inclined to dogma. It takes long to learn from experience or advice; affections and aversions are fixed and biased; in general the character proves more or less inaccessible.

As a person's mindfulness and concentration are both assumed to be weak, very little control over perceptual abilities is expected of him at the outset. The initial steps aim to make the meditator's mind pliable and receptive to the influence of wholesome qualities while loosening the ingrained control of the unwholesome factors. Initial practice is often difficult and even painful since the meditator's mind is unaccustomed to the kind of mental discipline demanded.

Meditation is, technically speaking, the consistent attempt to maintain a specific attentional set. For example, in the effort to keep his attention on the sensations of breathing, the meditator tries to keep his mind concentrated. His mind will not actually stay concentrated, but will wander to other thoughts and feelings. In practice he spends most of his time trying to *remember* to return his wandering mind to his breath, the object of concentration. The important thing is his attempt to concentrate on the breath.

In an alternate type of meditation, mindfulness, the meditator adopts a neutral stance toward whatever comes and goes in his stream of awareness, placing an equal value on whatever arises in his mind. No matter what might cross his mind, the meditator tries to maintain his mindfulness. His effort is not toward the generation of healthy factors per se. Because the healthy factors are the mental properties that keep his attention stable, they will come to dominate his mind as a by-product of his success in meditation. By learning to meditate with greater proficiency, the meditator at the same time increases the amount of healthy factors in his mental states.

The final achievement in meditation—nibbana or nirvana—is possible only when the meditator has developed the seven factors of enlightenment to a heightened degree. These factors are: mindfulness, wisdom, energy, rapture, calm, concentration, and equanimity. These seven factors are artfully balanced to speed the meditator's mind toward nibbana (Goldstein, 1976: p. 147):

> These are the seven qualities of enlightenment that have to be brought to maturity in our practice. Three of them are arousing factors, and three are tranquilizing ones. Wisdom, energy and rapture all arouse the mind; they make it wakeful and alert. Calm, concentration and equanimity tranquilize the mind and make it still. They all have to be in harmony: if there is too much arousal, the mind becomes restless; if too much tranquillity it goes to sleep. The factor of mindfulness is so powerful because it not only serves to awaken and strengthen all the other factors, but it also keeps them in their proper balance.

In Abhidhamma, nibbana is said to bring radical and lasting alteration of one's mental states. The significance for personality of nibbana is in its aftereffect. Unlike jhana, which has a short-lived effect on the meditator's personality, a person's post-nibbana personality is said to be irrevocably altered. A person's first experience of nibbana initiates a progression of changes which can finally lead to the point where unhealthy factors no longer occur. Not only are there no unhealthy factors in his states, but he has also eradicated any and all latent tendencies that could potentially lead to an unhealthy factor arising in his mind.

This transformation of consciousness is gradual. Though the experience of nibbana is always the same, as the meditator's insight strengthens he can attain nibbana at increasingly profound depths. At each successive level, groups of the unhealthy factors become totally inhibited. Finally not a single unhealthy factor will appear in any of the person's mental states. A meditator who reaches this point is called an *arahat.* He still, however, retains vestiges of his unique personality traits, as is evident from the vast range of personal style in stories of enlightened beings.

Arahat: Ideal Type of the Healthy Personality. The arahat embodies the essence of mental health in Abhidhamma. His personality traits are permanently altered; all his motives, perception, and actions that he formerly engaged in under the influence of unhealthy factors will have vanished. Rune Johansson, in *The Psychology of Nirvana* (1970), has culled Abhidhamma sources for the personality attributes of the arahat. His list includes:

- *absence of:* greed for sense desires; anxiety, resentments, or fears of any sort; dogmatisms such as the belief that this or that is "the Truth"; aversion to conditions such as loss, disgrace, pain, or blame; feelings of lust or anger; experiences of mental suffering; need for approval, pleasure, or praise; desire for anything for oneself beyond essential and necessary items; and

• *prevalence of:* impartiality toward others and equanimity in all circumstances; ongoing alertness and calm delight in experience no matter how ordinary or even seemingly boring; strong feelings of compassion and loving kindness; quick and accurate perception; composure and skill in taking action; openness to others and responsivity to their needs.

One of the few mentions of dreams in Abhidhamma suggests another unusual attribute of the arahat. People's dreams are said to be of four types. The first is due to some organic or muscular disturbance, and typically involves a strong physical sensation such as falling, flying, or being chased. Nightmares belong to this category. The second type of dream is due to one's activities during the day, and echoes these past experiences. Such dreams are generally mundane. The third kind of dream is of an actual event as it happens, akin to Jung's principle of synchronicity. The last type of dream is clairvoyant, an accurate prophecy of events yet to occur. When an arahat dreams, it is always such a clairvoyant dream (Van Aung, 1972). The Buddha was adept at interpreting symbols in his dreams, although there is no formal system for symbolic analysis in Abhidhamma. Just before his enlightenment, the Buddha had a series of vivid dreams that predicted his enlightenment, the teaching he would do afterward, the gathering of students to him, and the course of Buddhism after his death.

While the arahat may seem virtuous beyond belief from the perspective of Western psychology, he embodies characteristics common to the ideal type in most every Asian psychology. The arahat is the enlightened being, a prototype notable in the main by its absence in Western personality theory. But the arahat is an ideal type, the end-point in a gradual transformation which anyone can undertake, and in which anyone can succeed in whatever small measure. Thus the meditator may not become a saint overnight, but he may well experience himself changing so that he has a greater proportion of healthy mental states.

20. PSYCHOLOGY EAST
AND WEST

The arahat is easily recognized in almost any of the great world religions as the prototypical saint. Although Western religion still holds that possibility, Western psychology never has.

The Politics of Consciousness

The arahat represents a challenge to the paradigms of Western psychology. From the Western point of view, he is virtuous beyond belief. In our culture and in our psychology we have no such model for a radical transformation of consciousness of that sort: This level of human development overreaches the vision and goals of Western psychology. The arahat lacks many characteristics that Western psychology takes as givens of human nature; he seems too good to exist.

Where and when did the Western religious and psychological views of human possibilities begin to diverge? Virtually from the beginning of modern psychology. To a degree, psychology is autobiography: the personal history of theoreticians directly influencing their articulation of and emphasis in theory. Freud, for example, in his introduction to *Civilization and Its Discontents* tells of receiving a letter from the poet Romain Rolland, who had become a student of the great Indian saint Sri Ramakrishna. Rolland described a feeling of something "limitless and unbounded," which he saw as "the physiological basis of much of the wisdom of mysticism." Freud labeled the feeling "oceanic" and, admitting his puzzlement and failure to discover this oceanic feeling in himself, went on to reinterpret this fact of experience in a manner consonant with his own worldview, positing as its origin a feeling of infantile helplessness which he saw as the source of religious feeling.

In doing so, Freud explicitly applied a template which he had derived for understanding experience of a different order than Rolland was describing, but which seems to have rendered the data more comfortable for Freud, who noted: "The idea of men's receiving an intimation of their connection with the world around them through a feeling which is from the outset directed to that purpose sounds so strange and fits in so badly with the fabric of our psychology that one is justified in attempting to discover a psycho-analytic . . . explanation of such a feeling."

In the final words of this same introduction Freud articulated an attitude toward this and other aspects of altered states of consciousness which has since become an implicit assumption of many, if not most, of those who have followed in the psychoanalytic lineage he established: "It would not be hard to find connections here with a number of obscure modifications of mental life, such as trances or ecstacies. But I am moved to exclaim in the words of Schiller's diver: 'Let him rejoice who breathes up here in the roseate light' " (i.e., normal waking awareness).

William James had a retort for Freud's dismissing spiritual states out of hand. Although James didn't have Freud in mind, he referred to the same intellectual bent when he wrote (1961: p. 29):

> We're surely all familiar in a general way with this method of discrediting states of mind for which we have an antipathy. "Medical materialism" seems, indeed, a good appellation for the simple-minded system of thought which we are considering. Medical materialism finishes up St. Paul by calling his vision on the road to Damascus a discharging lesion of the occipital cortex, he being an epileptic. It snuffs out St. Teresa as an hysteric, St. Francis of Assisi as an hereditary degenerate. George Fox's discontent with the shams of his age and his pining for spiritual veracity, it treats as symptoms of a disordered colon. All such mental tensions, it says, are, when you come to the bottom of the matter, due to the perverted action of various glands which physiology will yet discover.

Consider how psychology, or the West for the most part, views spiritual life. We live in a culture that holds to the scientific worldview. In attempting to be a science, psychology has adapted that view with much benefit but at great cost. To become a psychologist means being socialized to have a negative attitude toward spiritual evolution or to be oblivious to that possibility.

The upshot is that, as a culture, one of the taboo topics that does not easily enter our collective consciousness is religious experience. In a mid-1970s "quality of life" survey of Americans, one question was, "Have you ever had the feeling of being very close to a powerful spiritual force that seemed to lift you out of yourself?" Forty percent replied that it had happened at least once; twenty percent said that it had happened several times; and five percent reported that it had happened often. Almost all of these people confessed they had never spoken to anyone—therapist, minister, priest, or rabbi—about their experiences. "They would think I was crazy" was the reason. Such experiences do not fit in with the Western worldview or religious worldview, let alone the psychological worldview. As a nation of "closet mystics," our theories of human possibility are, as a whole, very limited. We have a collective blind spot.

Perspectives on Reality

Individuals in each culture codify experience in terms of the categories of their own linguistic system, grasping reality only as it is presented in their code. Each culture punctuates and categorizes experience differently. The anthropologist recognizes that the study of a code different from our own can lead us to concepts and aspects of reality from which our own way of looking at the world excludes us.

Each culture has a specialized vocabulary in those areas of existence which are most salient to its own mode of experiencing the world. In this light it is intriguing that our own culture has as its major technical vocabulary for describing inner experience a highly specialized nosology of psychopathology, while Asian cultures such as India have equally intricate vocabularies for altered states of consciousness and stages in spiritual development.

Culture molds awareness to conform to certain norms, limits the types of experience or categories for experience available to the individual, and determines the appropriateness or acceptability of a given state of awareness or its communication in the social situation. As Goffman (1962) has shown, these principles apply to psychopathology in our own culture, and altered states of awareness may likewise be subject to the same influences. Western culture historically has been repressive of some altered states of consciousness, such as the gnostic heresies of the Middle Ages which led to the establishment of the Inquisition. In other contexts altered states have been encouraged, for example, the Ignatian Spiritual Exercises in Catholic monasticism.

Our normative cultural reality is state-specific. Insofar as "reality" is a consensually validated, but arbitrary, convention, an altered state of consciousness can represent an antisocial, unruly mode of being. As Ramanujan (1973) sees it, such an altered awareness constitutes an impropriety against an implicit cultural order, and so is "unmasking, undoing the manmade. It is an act of violation against ordinary expected loyalties, a breakdown of the predictable and secure." It is this same element of unpredictability that was one factor in formulating public policy of involuntary hospitalization for psychotics. Because altered states may subvert the social order in the same way, this same fear of the unpredictable may have been a major motivating force behind the repression in our own culture of means for inducing altered states—psychedelics, for instance—or for a more general suspicion of techniques such as meditation.

While the cultural value system that has led to the preeminence of the waking state and the preclusion of altered states (except for alcohol intoxication) from the cultural norm has proved functional in terms of, say, the gross national product and economic growth, they have also rendered us as a culture relatively unsophisticated in terms of altered states of consciousness. Other "primitive" and traditional cultures, while less materially productive than our own, are far more knowledgeable than we in the intricacies of consciousness. Some cultures explicitly educate some or all members in altering consciousness, and many have developed "technologies" for this purpose. The Bushmen are trained to enter a trance via dancing, and to use the trance state for healing (Katz, 1973); a Yaqui Indian "warrior" retrains his perceptual habits so as to apprehend messages and natural forces ordinarily unsensed; the Malaysian Senoi systematically utilize dream contents to maintain harmonious interpersonal relations in community life (Stewart, 1969).

Asian cultures have highly developed vocabularies for describing and delimiting distinct degrees, levels, and types of meditation-specific altered states which our own language only vaguely and clumsily can begin to approximate. Buddhist psychology enumerates eight distinct levels of *jhana,* while the English "concentration," "absorption," and "trance"—in combination our nearest approximation—miss the mark; the eighteen stages of awareness leading to nirvana described in the same system have no English equivalents whatsoever. Although English has borrowed the word "nirvana," its common usage is a distortion of what was originally denoted; though we have co-opted the concept, we have totally neglected the experience to which it refers. The experiential base of these Eastern teachings, however, may prove far more consequential for both our psychology and our culture than the concepts they offer.

Though Eastern and Western psychologies may partially overlap—in a common interest in attentional processes, or in an understanding of the nature of human suffering—each also thoroughly explores territory and techniques the other ignores or barely touches on. Psychoanalytic thought, for example, has charted aspects of what would be called "karma" in the East in far greater detail and complexity than any Eastern school of psychology, just as Eastern schools

have developed an array of techniques for voluntarily altering consciousness, and so established a technology for dealing with realities beyond the mind as it is conceptualized in
contemporary psychology or experienced in our usual state
of consciousness.

Psychologies East and West

Having described the vision, goal, and means of Buddhist
psychology, let us look at it from a Western point of view.
Who among psychologists in the West might appreciate
that kind of radical transformation? One likely candidate
was William James. In his *Principles of Psychology* he writes
(1950: p. 424):

> The faculty of voluntarily bringing back a wandering
> attention over and over again is the very root of judg-
> ment, character, and will. No one is *compos sui* if he
> have it not. An education which should improve this
> faculty would be the education par excellence.

James saw the virtue of retraining attention—the essence
of meditation—but adds, "It is easier to define this ideal than
to give practical directions for bringing it about."
Although "voluntarily bringing back a wandering attention" is the basic step in meditation, James was apparently
unaware that the training he recommended existed in Eastern psychologies. Even though James was familiar with
some aspects of Eastern philosophy, it is no surprise that he
was unaware of their psychologies. The majority of American psychologists have been by and large ignorant of these
Eastern psychologies. This is understandable in light of their
inaccessibility, until recently, to those who do not read Pali,

Sanskrit, or the other tongues in which they are found. In addition, when translated into English, these psychologies are rarely identified as such, being more often treated as religious doctrine. When called to the attention of the earlier personality theorists, like Freud, they were rejected out of hand.

Most Western personality theorists, however, have been oblivious even to the fact that Eastern psychologies like Abhidhamma exist. Even if these psychologies were brought to their attention, the likelihood is that most theorists would discount their validity on any of a number of counts. For the behaviorist, for example, a psychology such as those from the East would be rejected by virtue of its introspective, phenomenological nature. The behaviorist position is that inner experience cannot be studied scientifically and so no psychology can be found that is based on introspection.

Behaviorism in its infancy fought early battles with Titchener's Introspectionists, who held tenets quite similar to Abhidhamma: that consciousness is directly observable, is composed of describable units, and that the task of the psychologist is to analyze it into its components. In stating the behaviorist position, Watson (1913) was emphatic in his critique of the introspectionists, whom he contended had substituted "consciousness" for what was formerly called the soul: "The time seems to have come when psychology must discard all references to consciousness; when it need no longer delude itself into thinking that it is making of mental states the object of observation."

For the most part, Western psychologists have been reactive against Eastern psychologies. These psychologists have not perceived that these *are* psychologies. Instead, they view Eastern traditions as little more than muddled and fuzzy religious systems, totally devoid of matters that a hard-nosed psychologist ought to consider.

Commonalities Between Systems. A look at the mainstream models of sanity in Western psychology reveals an array of remarkable similarities to Eastern psychology. For example, Gordon Allport's (1968) depiction of maturity or mental health manifests such characteristics as realistic perception, self-acceptance or contentment with oneself, compassion, and warmth. There is no argument there—the two systems can be easily reconciled. But the Buddhist's system radically diverges from Allport's thought in regard to the latter's emphasis on strong ego-identity. One tenet of Buddhism holds that there is no abiding self, that ego itself is an illusion. This view marks the major disparity between the two.

Consider, too, Erik Erikson's (1963) final stage of maturity in the life cycle. Among the attributes of this stage are the acceptance of one's life circumstances, lack of resentment, and absence of fear (especially of death). Again, there is no argument with Buddhism—until Erikson adds ego-integrity, defending one's life-style, defending one's sense of self. If one has no enduring and unchanging self, what is there to defend?

One of the closer fits in Western psychology to the characteristics of the arahat is Abraham Maslow's (1971) self-actualized person. This person has a clear perception of reality, as well as spontaneity, detachment (relationships that are not clinging, intrusive, or possessive), independence from flattery, criticism, and compassion.

Another parallel comes from Ernest Becker's description of "character armor" (1969: pp. 83–84):

This makes . . . people remarkably stiff, as Reich saw, as though they actually wore armor. It makes them remarkably unsympathetic to points of view they have decided are not worth entertaining or too threatening to entertain. It shuts them off tightly from others who risk invading their world and upsetting it, even if they upset it by kindness and love. Love draws one out, breaks down barriers, places the human relationship on mutual terms. In a word, love takes relationships out of control of the armored person. It takes strength to live, simply because it takes strength to stand exposed without armor, open to the needs of others.

That, of course, is the posture of the arahat: undefended and open to the needs of others. In terms of an ideal type of "sanity," there is an overlap here with Buddhism.

A very remarkable commonality is found in an essay written forty years ago by Franz Alexander (1941). It has an unfortunate title: "Buddhistic Training as an Artificial Catatonia." Alexander, who trained at the Berlin Psychoanalytic Institute in the 1930s before coming to America, had access to translations of Buddhist texts from Pali into German. Unlike Freud, he actually studied these texts, and, unlike most Western psychologists, he was fascinated by what he found. Noting that the first stages of meditation involve an ascetic renunciation or turning away from the world, he concluded in psychoanalytic terms: "This symptomatic suppression of emotional life is actually the withdrawal of libido from the world, and directing it toward the body in 'a sadistic frenzy' which we all recognize clinically as melancholia."

Thus he saw the first stage of the progression of insight as melancholia. Regarding meditative absorption, he observed, "The person's own body and, indeed, his entire body, becomes the sole object. This feeling of pleasure, a consummate voluptuousness of all organs, tissues, and cells, a pleasure completely freed from the genitals, an orgasm diffused throughout the whole body, is a condition which we have described—the schizophrenic in his catatonic ecstasy."

According to Alexander, in meditation one moves from melancholia to catatonia. A further step, he proposed, consists of a constant diminution of the feeling of pleasure along with a gradual transition into apathy—the stage of indifference. He saw the final stage as a condition of complete mental emptiness and uniformity. Referring to nirvana, he concludes: "It is not difficult for us to recognize in this condition the last stage of schizophrenia—*schizophrenia dementia.*"

Despite his analytic tone, Alexander's analysis is not hostile. He saw a remarkable similarity between the progression of insight and a good psychoanalysis and saw the end goal of Buddhist absorption as an attempt at psychological regression to the condition of intrauterine life. The way to nirvana, he writes, can be likened to a film that is turning in reverse. He sees that the stages of insight actually peel back the stages of cognitive development into infancy, an idea more systematically developed by Daniel Brown (1977). He then points out the striking similarity between the psychoanalytic method and the doctrine of Buddha, i.e., the overcoming of effective resistance and narcissism, such that one is able to recollect the past instead of repeating it in a regression.

Alexander saw that something was going on in the Freudian and Buddhist approaches that were very similar. In his own writings Freud describes the attentional posture of the analyst in terms of "even-hovering attention." His description of the analyst's attentional stance makes it sound very similar to mindfulness meditation, or insight. Freud writes that this simply "consists in making no effort to concentrate the attention on anything in particular and maintaining in regard to all that one hears the same measure of calm and quiet attentiveness." In this sense, psychoanalysis is an interpersonal insight meditation: The client offers the stream of awareness and the analyst offers the witness—insightful, even-hovering attention.

There, though, the similarity in technique ends. In analysis the person does not go through the progression of insight as described in Abhidhamma. This would be seen as a digression. Although there is some commonality, psychoanalysis and psychotherapy in general hover at the lowest level of insight in the Buddhist model. They never proceed to the progression demanded by the Buddhist tradition to transform consciousness in a lasting manner.

West Meets East: Some History.   Asian psychology has proved remarkably durable, surviving longer than two thousand years; Western personality theories are quite young by comparison. Virtually every Eastern meditation system transplanted to the West—Transcendental Meditation, Zen, and the like—stems from this psychology or another much like it. But these recent arrivals are by no means the first dissemination of Eastern psychological theory to the West.

Western thinkers since the time of the Greeks and Romans have been influenced by Eastern philosophies. After all, Alexander (356–323 B.C.) and his armies founded kingdoms that spread well into north India, and both technologies and ideas traveled across Eurasia on the silk routes, centuries old even in Alexander's time. Plotinus (A.D. 205–270) was one of the early philosophers whose thought closely paralleled the psychological views of Eastern thinkers of his day. A native of Egypt of Roman descent, Plotinus went to Persia and India in A.D. 242 to study their philosophies. His ideas became the hallmark of Christian mystics for centuries after. Plotinus mapped out a world of experience beyond the bounds of sense reality, compared to which the normal world was illusory. In his theory a person could develop toward perfection by divorcing the "soul"—that is, the awareness that perceives through the senses, but not including the senses themselves—from their body. In doing so a person transcends self-awareness, time and place, to experience the ineffable One in a state of ecstacy. Plotinus' version of ecstacy agrees with such classical Indian texts as Patanjali's *Yoga Sutras,* which says that the person who can transcend the ordinary limits of the body, senses, and mind will enter an altered state of ecstatic union with God. This same doctrine became part of Christian psychology, surfacing in one form or another within the influential writings of the Egyptian St. Antony (Waddell, 1957), St. John of the Cross (1958), and Meister Eckhardt, to name a few.

With the rise of the natural sciences, the positivistic approach came to dominate Western science and philosophy. To progressive thinkers the mystical aspects of religion—if not religion itself—fell out of fashion. Western psychology has its roots in the positivist tradition, and by and large the early psychologists turned to concerns other than those of the religious mystics. By the nineteenth century Eastern thought had less impact on the fledgling psychologies of the time than on the philosophers and poets. The writings of the Transcendentalists, such as Emerson and Thoreau, and the poetry of Walt Whitman, are permeated with the words and concepts of the East. William James, America's most prominent nineteenth-century psychologist, was keenly interested in religion, both Eastern and Western. He befriended Vivekananda, an Indian Swami who toured America after speaking at the First World Congress of Religions in 1893. Religion and the occult fascinated James; his book *Varieties of Religious Experience* (1961) remains a classic on the psychology of religion. But because Eastern thought is largely religious, the scientific bent of modern psychology has lead the great majority of Western psychologists to ignore the teachings of their Eastern counterparts.

One reason why some Western psychologists have become interested in Eastern theories is that they deal in part with a range of experience that our own theorists have largely ignored. A well-recorded instance is the case of the Canadian psychiatrist R. M. Bucke. His experience occurred during a visit to England in 1872; one account tells us (Bucke, 1969: p. iii):

> He and two friends had spent the evening reading Wordsworth, Shelley, Keats, Browning, and especially Whitman. They parted at midnight, and he had a long drive in a hansom. His mind, deeply under the influence of the ideas, images and emotions called up by the reading and the talk of the evening, was calm and peaceful. He was in a state of quiet, almost passive, enjoyment.
>
> All at once, without warning of any kind, he found himself wrapped around, as it were, by a flame-colored cloud. For an instant he thought of fire—some sudden conflagration in the great city. The next [instant] he knew that the light was within himself.
>
> Directly after there came upon him a sense of exultation, of immense joyousness, accompanied or immediately followed by an intellectual illumination quite impossible to describe.

Afterward Bucke was to speak of his experience as a glimpse of "cosmic consciousness," a phrase Walt Whitman, the nineteenth-century American poet, borrowed from the Vedantic philosophy of India, and which Bucke in turn appropriated. In using this Eastern concept to interpret his unusual psychological state, Bucke was one of the first to turn Eastward to understand aspects of the mind about which Western psychologies have little to say. The psychology of Bucke's time provided no labels save those of psychopathology for such states as he entered that night. The modern interest in Eastern psychologies may be due in part to the increasing frequency of experiences of altered states, like Bucke's, that our psychological theories do not deal with. Our present psychologies have little to say about such states—whether induced by drugs, meditation, or other means—that resonates with the experience of the person who undergoes them. Many Eastern psychologies offer ways to understand altered states that can make sense of these often confusing experiences.

Among modern personality theorists, Carl Jung was probably the most knowledgeable about Eastern psychologies. Jung was a close friend of the Indologist Heinrich Zimmer and was himself an authority on the mandala, a central motif in much sacred art of the East. Jung wrote forewords to books by the Zen scholar D. T. Suzuki (1974), and by Richard Wilhelm, translator of the *I Ching* and other Chinese Taoist texts. Jung also penned commentaries on Evans-Wentz' translations of *The Tibetan Book of the Great Liberation* (1969) and *The Tibetan Book of the Dead* (1969), two important works in the psychological compendium of Tibetan Buddhism. Jung's friend and neighbor, Herman Hesse, spread Eastern thought through his novels *Siddhartha* (1970) and *Journey to the East* (1971). Jung reached into matters alien to positivistic science by his extensive analysis of Eastern religions. Although he also warned of the dangers for a Westerner of being engulfed by Eastern traditions, Jung's writings form a major bridge between the psychologies of the East and West.

The work of Carl Jung shows him to be far more informed about the Eastern psychologies than Freud was. Despite his familiarity with the psychologies of the East, Jung was harshly critical of Europeans who tried to apply Eastern teachings to themselves. He felt it was too easy to become fascinated by the exotic forms of the East as a means of avoiding one's own problems (1968, pp. 99–101):

> People will do anything, no matter how absurd, in order to avoid facing their own souls. They will practice yoga and all its exercises, observe a strict regimen of diet, learn theosophy by heart, or mechanically repeat mystic texts from the literature of the whole world—all because they cannot get on with themselves and have not the slightest faith that anything useful could ever come out of their own souls.

Jung diligently studied the Eastern psychologies, chastising those who indulged in them with more than a scholarly interest. He may have also wanted to draw criticism away from his own theories and methods. Jung's exploration into the human psyche and the use of mandalas, the *I Ching,* and other tools made him appear to some of his contemporaries as mad as any Eastern mystic. Jung retorted, rather testily (1968, pp. 101–102):

> I have no wish to disturb such people at their pet pursuits, but when anybody who expects to be taken seriously is deluded enough to think that I use yoga methods and yoga doctrines or that I get my patients, whenever possible, to draw mandalas for the purpose of bringing them to the "right point"—then I really must protest and tax these people with having read my writings with the most horrible inattention.

Another source of Jung's resistance stemmed from his own ideas about the function of religion. To Jung, religions develop as a means for humans to know the archetypes—those potentialities for action and thought that inhere in the very structure of the human psyche. The Eastern religions, he felt, represented a higher level of development that reflected the maturity of the ancient civilizations of Asia. Europe and its indigenous faiths were younger and thus less sophisticated. As a person must go through each developmental stage to achieve full maturity, so must each race. It was unnatural for Europeans to turn to disciplines such as yoga, for these methods reflected a uniquely Eastern history and experience.

However, Jung did not reject the goal of the Eastern psychologies; he simply objected to their method as unsuited to the Western mind. He identified the altered state that a yogi seeks in trance (or *samadhi*) as an absorption in the collective unconscious, the deepest layer of the psyche and the realm of the archetypes. Jung believed that his own method of individuation led to the same goal: a shift away from the ego and toward the self. In his essay on "Yoga and the West," Jung shows his respect for this Eastern psychology; at the same time he does not endorse it as a method for the West: "I say to whomsoever I can: Study yoga—you will learn an infinite amount from it—but do not try to apply it, for we Europeans are not so constituted that we apply these methods correctly, just like that" (1958, p. 534). Rather than borrowing an unsuitable yoga from the East, said Jung, we should find our own path (1958, p. 483):

Instead of learning the spiritual techniques of the East by heart and imitating them in a Christian way—*imitatio Christi!*—with a correspondingly forced attitude, it would be far more to the point to find out whether there exists in the unconscious an introverted tendency similar to that which has become the guiding spiritual principle of the East. We should then be in a position to build on our own ground with our own methods.

Apart from Jung, the Eastern psychologies have made their greatest inroads in the West through their influence on the holistic outlooks of such theorists as Angyal and Maslow, the humanists Buber and Fromm, the existentialist Boss, and the wave of "transpersonal psychologists" (Tart, 1976). Maslow, for example, read extensively in Eastern literature, and Buber, Fromm, and Boss have each had a personal history of contact with Eastern teachers. Buber knew the works of the Hasidic masters, the mystics of Judaism. Fromm has had a long-standing dialogue with Buddhist teachers; his *Zen Buddhism and Psychoanalysis* (1970) was co-authored with D. T. Suzuki, an experienced Zen student and scholar, as well as with Richard DeMartino, a professor of religion.

Medard Boss, the influential Swiss existentialist, was invited to lecture on psychiatry in India, where he had an opportunity to meet Indian holy men. Feeling that Western therapies lack the ability to bring an illuminating insight of power comparable to that of Eastern methods, he looked to the traditions of India for guidance. Boss was little impressed with those Westerners he met who had donned the garb of Indian holy men; he found them to have inflated their egos with Indian formulas of wisdom, but otherwise to be unchanged, not having truly incorporated these formulas into their own existence. The Indian sages he met, however, impressed him deeply (1965, pp. 187–188):

And yet there were the exalted figures of the sages and holy men themselves, each one of them a living example of the possibility of human growth and maturity and of the attainment of an imperturbable inner peace, a joyous freedom from guilt, and a purified, selfless goodness and calmness. . . . No matter how carefully I observe the waking lives of the holy men, no matter how ready they were to tell me about their dreams, I could not detect in the best of them a trace of a selfish action or any kind of repressed or consciously concealed shadow life.

Boss came away from these meetings with the conviction that, in light of the teachings and behavior of the Eastern masters, the methods and aims of Western psychotherapy were inadequate. Compared with the degree of self-purification Eastern discipline demands, "even the best Western training analysis is not much more than an introductory course." Nevertheless, in Boss' view, the Western "yogis" in whom he was so disappointed could all have benefited by a psychoanalysis as preparation for their further training in Eastern disciplines. The Italian psychiatrist Alberto Assagioli would agree with Boss' assessment of the relationship between Western therapies and Eastern disciplines. Assagioli's (1971) "psychosynthesis" offers a wide-ranging set of therapeutic methods that start by dealing with a person's physical problems—especially psychosomatic disorders—proceed through his or her psychological disturbances, and finally culminate in spiritual exercises.

Alan Watts, though not himself a psychological theorist, did much to bring Eastern teachings to the awareness of Western psychologists as a guest lecturer at numerous medical schools, hospitals, and psychiatric institutes, and in a series of books, most importantly, *Psychotherapy East and West* (1961). Watts recognized that what he called Eastern "ways of liberation" resemble Western psychotherapy in that both are concerned with changing peoples' feelings about themselves and their relation to others and to the world of nature. Western therapies, for the most part, deal with disturbed people; Eastern disciplines with normal, socially adjusted people. Even so, Watts saw that the aims of the ways of liberation were compatible with the therapeutic goals of several theorists, notably Jung's individuation, Maslow's self-actualization, Allport's functional autonomy, and Adler's creative selfhood.

Some ten years after the appearance of Watts' book comparing Eastern disciplines and Western therapies, a book by Abraham Maslow (1971) was published posthumously that indirectly carried Watts' work a step further. Maslow, about a year before his death, had suffered a near-fatal heart attack. After recovering from this brush with death, he set about to organize and re-think his major contributions to personality theory. One product of his effort was an essay called "Theory Z" in which he postulated a degree of healthiness more "fully human" than any he had described heretofore. These "self-actualizing transcenders" are people who, by his description, sound like the ideal types of fully healthy people in Eastern psychologies. Although Maslow cites no single Eastern psychologist as a source for his ideas, he freely sprinkles Eastern concepts in his discussion, for example, calling a therapist at the level of Theory Z, among other terms, a "Taoistic guide," a "Guru," a "Boddhisattva," and a "Tsaddik," all names in Eastern traditions for a sage or saint. It is almost certain that Maslow developed his new concept of healthiness independently, assimilating bits of Eastern psychologies as they fit his own thinking. It seems unlikely that he studied any of the Eastern schools with the intention of borrowing their concepts.

The same posthumous volume contains an essay in which Maslow presents a new perspective on an earlier book *Religions, Values, and Peak-experiences* (1964). In this essay he cautioned against those who might exalt the "peak experience" as an end in itself or might turn away from the world in a romantic search: "The great lesson from the true mystics . . . that the sacred is *in* the ordinary, that it is to be found in one's daily life, in one's neighbors, friends, and family, in one's back yard, and that travel may be a *flight* from confronting the sacred—this lesson can be easily lost." Here again he echoes the Eastern psychologies by recognizing both the value and the hard work required for what he calls "the plateau experience" (1971, pp. 348–349):

> Plateau experiencing can be achieved, learned, earned by long hard work. . . . A transient glimpse is certainly possible in the peak experiences which may, after all, come sometimes to anyone. But, so to speak, to take up residence on the high plateau . . . that is another matter altogether. That tends to be a lifelong effort.

A close collaborator of Maslow's, Anthony Sutich, founded a psychology journal in 1969 devoted to the study of the kind of concepts Maslow described. Sutich's *Journal of Transpersonal Psychology* has become the forum for psychologists with interests similar to Maslow's; "Theory Z" was first published there, and Maslow himself was a founding member of the Board of Editors. While there is no single spokesman for the transpersonal perspective, as a whole this group of psychologists is most open to studying and borrowing from Eastern psychologies. Sutich's statement (1969) in the first issue of the *Journal* expresses the far-ranging interests of transpersonal psychology (p. 1):

> Transpersonal Psychology is the title given to an emerging force in the psychology field by a group ... who are interested in those ultimate human capacities and potentialities that have no systematic place in ... behavioristic theory ("first force"), classical psychoanalytic theory ("second force"), or Humanistic psychology ("third force"). The emerging Transpersonal Psychology ("fourth force") is concerned specifically with ... ultimate values, unitive consciousness, peak experiences, ecstasy, mystical experience, awe, being, self-actualization, essence, bliss, wonder, ultimate meaning, transcendence of the self, spirit, oneness, cosmic awareness ... and related concepts, experiences, and activities.

Because psychologists with a transpersonal orientation deal with phenomena such as "awe" and "unitive consciousness," they often turn to the Eastern psychologies for guidance, just as R. M. Bucke did a century ago. One area where some see Western psychologies as deficient relative to those from the East is in dealing with human spiritual aspirations or religious life. Charles Tart, a major investigator of altered states of consciousness (1969), edited a pioneering collection of these Eastern theories in *Transpersonal Psychologies* (1976). Tart observes that Eastern psychologies do not share the assumptions of Western theories and so do not suffer the same limitations (1976, p. 5):

> Orthodox, Western psychology has dealt very poorly with the spiritual side of man's nature, choosing either to ignore its existence or to label it pathological. Yet

much of the agony of our time stems from a spiritual vacuum. Our culture, our psychology, has ruled out man's spiritual nature, but the cost of this attempted suppression is enormous. If we want to find ourselves, our spiritual side, it's imperative for us to look at the psychologies that have dealt with it.

Tart suggests that the realm of spiritual experience is connected to the realm of altered states of consciousness. To the extent that the Eastern psychologies help us predict or control such altered states, the psychologies are themselves state-specific sciences, that is, theories that derive from and apply to specific states of awareness. Tart's purpose in surveying the transpersonal psychologies of the East is not to offer them for wholesale adoption by Western psychology, but to consider them as guides for our own efforts. He proposes that we can use Eastern thought to build, in the mode of contemporary science, a more fully informed understanding of these spiritual realms and the altered awareness they bring. Tart cautions: "I have no doubt that many sacred scriptures contain a great deal of valuable information and wisdom, and I am certain that many spiritual teachers have a great deal to teach us that is of immense value, but even the greatest sorts of spiritual teachings must be adapted to the culture of the people they are presented to if they are really to connect with their whole psyches" (1976, p. 58). Tart envisions "the development of scientific tradition with the vast, uncharted [to science] sea of human potentials we can call man's spiritual potentialities."

Perhaps the most sophisticated integration of psychologies East and West to date is emerging from the work of Western scholars who have immersed themselves in Eastern disciplines and combined these insights with those of mainstream psychology. A pioneering effort in this tradition is *Transfor-*

mations of Consciousness (1986), with contributions from Ken Wilber, Jack Engler, Daniel P. Brown, and Mark Epstein. Their work combines the major Western clinical understanding of psychological development with the theories of the East, showing how they fit together in a complementary vision of human possibilities. This work marks a new epoch in the dialogue between these psychologies, one in which the two streams of thought meet in mutual respect and understanding.

21. MEDITATION: RESEARCH AND PRACTICAL APPLICATIONS

Meditation and Stress

While I was in India in 1971, I met a number of Indian yogis, Tibetan lamas, and Buddhist monks. I was struck by the relaxed warmth, openness, and alertness of these men and women, no matter what the situation. Each was the kind of person I enjoyed being with, and I felt nourished when I left them.

There were vast differences in their beliefs and backgrounds. The one thing they shared was meditation. Then I met S. N. Goenka, a teacher who was not a monk, but an industrialist who had been one of the richest men in Burma. Though he had been highly successful, Goenka found that his hectic pace took its toll in the form of daily migraine headaches. Medical treatments at European and American clinics had no effect on his headaches, and he turned to meditation as a last resort. Within three days of his first instruction, his migraines disappeared.

In the 1960s there was a military coup in Burma, and the new socialist government seized all of Goenka's holdings, leaving him nearly penniless. He emigrated to India, where he took advantage of old business and family connections to start a new business. While his new enterprise was getting underway, he traveled throughout India giving 10-day courses in meditation. Some reservoir of energy allowed him to be both full-time meditation teacher and businessman. His example helped me to see that one needn't be a monk to meditate. You can separate the physical effects of meditation from its monastic context.

When I returned to Harvard from India, I found that psychologist Gary Schwartz had begun research into meditation. He had found that meditators reported much lower daily anxiety levels than nonmeditators. They had many fewer psychological or psychosomatic problems such as colds, headaches, and sleeplessness.

My personal experience, and these scientific findings, suggested that meditators were able to roll with life's punches, handling daily stresses well and suffering fewer consequences from them. With Schwartz as my thesis advisor, I designed a study to see how the practice of meditation helps one cope with stress.

I had two groups of volunteers come to our physiology lab. One group consisted of meditation teachers, all of whom had been meditating for at least two years. The other group of people were interested in meditation but had not yet begun to meditate. Once in the lab, each volunteer was told to sit quietly and either relax or meditate. If nonmeditators were assigned to the meditation treatment, I taught them how to meditate right there in the lab. After 20 minutes of relaxation or meditation, the volunteers saw a short film depicting a series of bloody accidents among workers in a woodworking shop. The film is a standard way

of inducing stress during laboratory studies, because everyone who watches it is upset by the accidents depicted in the
film.

The meditators had a unique pattern of reaction to the
film. Just as the accident was about to happen, their heart
rates increased and they began to sweat more than the nonmeditators. To get ready to meet the distressing sight, their
heartbeats rose and their bodies mobilized in what physiolo-
gists call the fight-or-flight reaction. But as soon as the
accident was over, the meditators recovered, their signals of
bodily arousal falling more quickly than those of nonmeditators. After the film, they were more relaxed than the
nonmeditators, who still showed signs of tension.

This pattern of greater initial arousal and faster recovery
showed up in experienced meditators whether or not they
had meditated before the movie began. In fact, the meditators felt more relaxed the whole time they were in the lab.
Rapid recovery from stress is a typical trait of meditators.
Even the novices, who meditated for the first time that day
in the lab, were less anxious after the film and recovered
more quickly than the nonmeditators.

Meditation itself seems the most likely cause of rapid
stress recovery. If the rapid recovery among experienced
meditators had been the result of some personality trait
common to the kind of people who stick with meditation,
the novices would have been as slow to recover as were the
people who relaxed.

My study may explain the lower incidence of anxiety and
psychosomatic disorders among meditators. People who are
chronically anxious or who have a psychosomatic disorder
share a specific pattern of reaction to stress; their bodies
mobilize to meet the challenge, then fail to stop reacting
when the problem is over. The initial tensing up is essential,
for it allows them to marshal their energy and awareness to

deal with a potential threat. But their bodies stay aroused for danger when they should be relaxed, recouping spent energies and gathering resources for the next brush with stress.

The anxious person meets life's normal events as though they were crises. Each minor happening increases his tension, and his tension in turn magnifies the next ordinary event—a deadline, an interview, a doctor's appointment—into a threat. Because the anxious person's body stays mobilized after one event has passed, he has a lower threat threshold for the next. Had he been in a relaxed state, he would have taken the second event in stride.

A meditator handles stress in a way that breaks up the threat-arousal-threat spiral. The meditator relaxes after a challenge passes more often than the nonmeditator. This makes him unlikely to see innocent occurrences as harmful. He perceives threat more accurately, and reacts with arousal only when necessary. Once aroused, his rapid recovery makes him less likely than the anxious person to see the next deadline as a threat.

Effects of Meditation on the Brain. The popular appeal of meditation is the promise of becoming more relaxed more of the time. But some highly pressured members of society are not sure that relaxation is a good thing. When Harvard Medical School's Herbert Benson wrote an article in the *Harvard Business Review* urging businesses to give employees time for a meditation break, there was a flood of letters protesting that stress and tension were essential to good business management. A friend of mine, when told to meditate to lower his blood pressure, responded: "I need to take it easy, but I don't want to become a zombie."

Fortunately, meditation doesn't make zombies. The meditation experts I met in India and America were among the most lively people I've met anywhere. Research into the effects of meditation on the brain may suggest why.

Meditation trains the capacity to pay attention. This sets it apart from other ways of relaxing, most of which let the mind wander as it will. This sharpening of attention lasts beyond the meditation session itself. It shows up in a number of ways in the rest of the meditator's day. Meditation, for example, has been found to improve one's ability to pick up subtle perceptual cues in the environment, and to pay attention to what is going on rather than letting the mind wander elsewhere. These skills mean that in conversation with another person, the meditator should be more empathic. Because the meditator can pay sharper attention to what the other person is doing and saying, he can pick up more of the hidden messages the other is sending.

TM and Gurdjieff Techniques. All meditation techniques seem to be equally effective ways to lower the anxiety level and help handle stress. But different types of meditation retrain attention in different ways.

Some of my colleagues at Harvard—Gary Schwartz, Richard Davidson, and Richard Margolin—compared people trained in Transcendental Meditation (TM) with a group trained in a Gurdjieffian technique. This technique is named after G. I. Gurdjieff, the turn-of-the-century Russian who brought to the West an amalgam of esoteric meditative techniques he collected on his Asian travels.

In TM the meditator listens in his mind to a Sanskrit sound, repeatedly starting the sound going mentally each time his mind wanders. The Gurdjieff training, like TM, includes techniques that improve the capacity to keep a single, subtle thought in mind. But Gurdjieff's students also apply this improved power of attention to learning an intricate series of dancelike movements, and to sensing specific areas throughout the body.

The Harvard group tested the TM and the Gurdjieff meditators one by one. They looked at brain-wave patterns while the meditator concentrated on the sensations in his own right hand, and then on a picture of someone sitting in a laboratory chair. The psychologists recorded signals from the part of the brain that controls vision and from the part that controls muscle movement. They found that when a Gurdjieff meditator attended to his hand, the muscle-movement center in his brain became active, as though preparing to order a movement. At the same time, the visual area of the brain became less active. When a Gurdjieff student looked at the picture, the opposite happened; the visual area became more active, the motor area quiet. No such differences appeared among the TM group, nor in a group of people who had never had meditation training of any kind.

The Gurdjieff meditators' brains showed cortical specificity, the ability to turn on those areas of the brain necessary to the task at hand while leaving the irrelevant areas inactive.

This is the way the brain works when we are at our most efficient and alert. If too many areas are aroused too much, we get overexcited and perform poorly. If too few areas are active, we're groggy. The machinery of the brain and body works best when only those areas that are essential to the work at hand are activated. The Gurdjieff training developed this ability, while TM did not.

Both TM and Gurdjieff training prime the power of attention while relaxing the body. But only the Gurdjieff training applies this relaxed alertness to improving skills of sensory detection and muscle control. This same training combination is found in many Eastern martial arts. If his mind wandered, the karate master would break his hand, not the brick. Powerful concentration amplifies the effectiveness of any kind of activity.

The research evidence shows that one meditation technique is about as good as another for improving the way we handle stress. Meditators become more relaxed the longer they have been at it. At the same time they become more alert, something other ways to relax fail to bring about because they do not train the ability to pay attention.

Healing Properties of Meditation

In 1984 the National Institute of Health (NIH) released a consensus report that recommended meditation (along with salt and dietary restrictions) above prescription drugs as the first treatment for mild hypertension. This official recognition was a catalyst in the spread of meditation and other relaxation techniques as treatments in medicine and psychotherapy.

In the early 1970s, when I did my dissertation research on meditation and relaxation as antidotes to stress reactivity (Goleman and Schwartz, 1976), this idea was new. I found that meditation lowered anxiety levels and sped the meditator's recovery from stress arousal. The clinical applications for stress disorders seemed obvious.

I was not alone in my findings. The mid–1970s saw a flood of research on meditation, particularly its health benefits (see Shapiro and Walsh, 1984, for the most complete survey). The methodological rigor of these studies was, frankly, uneven. But the thrust of the findings was clear: meditation was helpful in many ways. For instance, the regular practice of meditation lessened the frequency of colds and headaches and reduced the severity of hypertension. Although these medical applications received some attention, the stronger initial welcome for meditation came from psychotherapists who saw it as a way for patients to manage anxiety without drugs, to gain access to otherwise blocked memories and feelings, and as a general prescription for handling garden-variety stress. Meditation was a stress management tool par excellence and was vigorously marketed as such to schools, hospitals, and businesses, along with a variety of other relaxation techniques.

Meditation and relaxation are not one and the same; meditation is, in essence, the effort to retrain attention. This gives meditation its unique cognitive effects, such as increasing the meditator's concentration and empathy. The most common use of meditation, however, is as a quick-and-easy relaxation technique.

Although the Eastern roots of meditation were exotic, it became apparent to investigators that, in terms of its metabolic effects, meditation shared much in common with home-grown techniques of relaxation such as Edmund Jacobsen's progressive relaxation and muscle tension biofeedback, and with European imports such as autogenic training. Meditation differed from other relaxation techniques in its attentional components, as Herbert Benson (1975) pointed out in his best-seller *The Relaxation Response,* but much of its therapeutic quality lied in its effectiveness in getting the meditator into a state of deep relaxation.

As research on relaxation techniques for the management of stress disorders continues, the evidence of their effectiveness has become more compelling. The neuroendocrine changes brought about by becoming deeply relaxed have turned out to be more profound than was first believed by earlier investigators who viewed relaxation techniques mostly in terms of their relief of muscle tension and mental worry. More biologically sophisticated investigations have revealed profound effects on immune function as well as a range of other changes with specific clinical applications.

For instance, Janice Kiecolt-Glaser (1984, 1985) found that elderly residents of a retirement home who used a relaxation exercise showed a significant increase in the strength of their immune defenses against tumors and viruses. Medical students who used these techniques during the stress of exams showed increased levels of helper cells that defend against infectious disease. The discovery of these changes explains earlier reports that meditation, for example, increased resistance to colds and flus.

Perhaps the earliest and strongest medical interest in relaxation has been its assistance in fighting heart disease. Researchers working with Dr. Benson reported that meditation decreased the body's response to norepinephrine, a hormone released in reaction to stress. Although norepinephrine ordinarily stimulates the cardiovascular system, increasing blood pressure, it did not have its usual effect in the meditators. Instead, the meditators showed a decrease in blood pressure. This response mimics that of the beta-blockers prescribed to control blood pressure.

The clinical use of relaxation to control high blood pressure, especially mild cases, has become a well-established treatment, as the NIH report reflects; if practiced faithfully, it can often replace medication or lessen the reliance on drugs. In a British study, patients trained in these methods were found to have lower blood pressure four years after the training ended (Patel et al., 1985).

The benefits for heart disease patients go far beyond controlling blood pressure. Relaxation has been found to help relieve suffering from angina and arrythmia and to lower blood cholesterol levels. Dean Ornish (1983) has shown that relaxation training enhances blood flow to the heart, lessening the danger of silent ischemia.

Diabetics, too, can benefit from relaxation. Richard Surwit (1983) found that relaxation training improved the regulation of glucose in patients with adult-onset diabetes. Using Jacobsen's progressive relaxation with asthmatics, Paul Lehrer (1986) found that the practice lessened the emotional reactions that often preceded attacks and improved the flow in constricted airway passages.

For pain patients, some forms of relaxation offer particular promise. Jon Kabat-Zinn (1985) found that mindfulness meditation, coupled with yoga, lowered the reliance on pain-killers and lessened the level of pain in chronic pain sufferers. The causes of the pain ranged from backaches and headaches (migraine and tension) to the various cases seen in pain clinics. Four years after the training ended, the benefits still held.

Relaxation techniques of all kinds are being used by medical patients of different kinds, particularly where stress plays a causative role or exacerbates the problem—and there are few cases where it does not. Some of the more promising applications are seen with the side effects of kidney dialysis and cancer chemotherapy, gastrointestinal disorders, insomnia, emphysema, and skin disorders.

Relaxation is also widely used as an adjunct in psychotherapy, where it has been well accepted far longer than it has in medicine. Even so, there are some problems in applying these techniques. A few people react to relaxation with increased tension and even panic (Cohen, 1985). In these cases, relaxation may need to be introduced after special cognitive preparation or simply not at all.

There are other situations in which meditation may not be appropriate for patients. A schizoid may possibly worsen reality-testing, becoming overly absorbed in inner realities; those in acute emotional states might be too agitated to begin meditation; obsessive-compulsives might on the one hand be too closed to new experience to try meditation, or on the other, overzealous in their efforts.

One task ahead is to sort out the significant differences, if any, between relaxation and meditation techniques in terms of the people and problems for which they will be most effective. But, as the research evidence makes clear, these methods offer a powerful way to tap the inner capacity of patients to participate in their own healing.

Meditation and Psychotherapy

Hans Selye (1978) points to the need for a "stress therapy" which would function not against any one disease producer or ameliorate any specific symptom, but rather would be preventive, working in a manner favorable to the organism as a whole. The pattern of stress reactivity I found among meditators is one in which the meditator is more alert but composed in response to threat cues, and recovers more efficiently. To the degree that the recovery phase of stress is the key to chronic anxiety symptoms and psychosomatic disorders, meditation may function as a stress therapy, on the psychologic as well as the purely somatic levels, facilitating more rapid recovery from stress situations. As such, meditation may prove a useful adjunct to any psychotherapy.

Other processes of meditation may coincide with aspects of therapy. For example, as the meditator turns his attention inward he becomes keenly aware of thoughts, feelings, and states drawn from the stored pool of his total experience which arise spontaneously. Since the meditator is at the same time deeply relaxed, the whole contents of his mind can be seen as composing a "desensitization hierarchy." This hierarchy is not limited to those items which therapist and patients have identified as problematic, though these are certainly included, but extends to all one's life concerns, to whatever is "on one's mind." In this sense, meditation may be natural, global self-desensitization.

This may account for the lessening of tension usually associated with repressed material when meditation has been used as an adjunct to therapy, thus allowing formerly painful material to surface with greater awareness. After meditating, the patient's free association has been found particu larly rich in content while at the same time the patient is more able to tolerate this material. In this way meditation seems to improve access to the unconscious.

Many contemporary therapies begin from an understanding of the human condition similar in certain respects to that of Abhidhamma. Freud, for example, saw the "universal neurosis in man," Buddha saw that "all worldings are deranged." While the insight was similar, the response differed. Freud sought through analysis to help his patients face, understand, and reconcile themselves to this "tragic" condition of life. Buddha sought through meditation to eradicate the sources of suffering in a radical reorientation of consciousness.

Psychodynamic therapy since Freud has worked within the constraints of consciousness to alter the impact of the contents of one's past as it effects the present. Asian psychologies have largely ignored the *contents* of awareness, while seeking to alter the *context* in which they are registered in awareness.

Conventional psychotherapies assume as givens the mechanisms underlying mental processes, while seeking to alter them at the level of socially conditioned patterns. Asian systems disregard these same socially conditioned patterns, while aiming at the control and self-regulation of the underlying mechanisms themselves.

Therapies break the hold of past conditioning on present

behavior; meditation aims to alter the process of conditioning per se so that it will no longer be a prime determinant of future acts. In the Asian approach behavioral and personality change is secondary, an epiphenomenon of changes, through the voluntary self-regulation of mental states, in the basic processes which define our reality.

Consciousness is the medium which carries the messages that compose experience. Psychotherapies are concerned with these messages and their meanings; meditation instead directs itself to the nature of the medium, consciousness. These two approaches are by no means mutually exclusive; rather, they are complementary. A therapy of the future may integrate techniques from both approaches, possibly producing a change in the whole person more thoroughgoing and more potent than either in isolation.

Meditation and Consciousness Research: Some Proposals

As discussed earlier, there are two fundamental attentional strategies in meditation: concentration and mindfulness. The state reached by the meditator depends on the method used. Concentration leads the meditator to become one-pointed and finally merge his attention with its object. Mindfulness leads the meditator to witness the workings of his own mind, coming to perceive with detachment the finer segments of his stream of thought. The altered states produced by each approach are radically different.

While these two attentional routes to altered states represent prototypes, they do not exhaust all the possible changes in consciousness that meditation can bring. Attentional manipulation can be linked with other practices such as movement, controlled breathing, or fasting. The addition of other practices compounds the complexity of the calculus for changes in awareness.

The classical literature on the phenomenology of meditation draws a distinction between altered *states* and altered *traits* of consciousness. Altered states are temporary and typically occur within the range of the meditator's activity—the trances called *samadhi* in Sanskrit and *jhana* in Pali. Altered traits are ongoing transformations in the nature of the meditator's consciousness and persist no matter what activity he may be engaged in. Meditative altered states last only as long as a particular attentional maneuver (such as one-pointedness) is pursued and diminish rapidly when the effort ceases. Altered traits are changes in consciousness that have become habitual and effortless; thus, they are an automatic feature of the person's baseline states of consciousness. They remain after the initial effort ceases.

Research on Meditation and Consciousness.   While research on meditation to date has been largely piecemeal, it tends to confirm the broad strokes of the state and trait changes in consciousness described in classical sources. But none of the research conclusively supports these claims, in part because of sampling bias and other methodological problems (see J. M. Davidson, 1976; Shapiro, 1980; Schuman, 1980) and because crucial measures have never been made.

State changes during meditation have been one major research focus. The classical literature makes clear that the state produced by meditation depends on the specifics of the attentional manipulation involved. One-pointedness techniques, for example, should produce a narrowing of awareness, reaching at its most fully focused point an altered state in which the meditator is oblivious to all external stimuli. Mindfulness techniques should produce a state of ongoing awareness to stimuli with no habituation of the orienting response.

Two of the earliest studies of meditation seem to have confirmed these classical hypotheses. Anand and his associates (Anand et al., 1961) brought a portable EEG unit to India and measured an obliging yogi who claimed he could enter a state of samadhi. During meditation, his EEG showed a strong, continuous alpha rhythm. When the researchers made loud noises and even touched the yogi's arm with a hot test tube, there purportedly was no break in the alpha rhythm. The yogi's failure to show alpha blocking to a strong stimulus suggests that, indeed, he was in a state of samadhi, oblivious to external stimuli.

Kasamatsu and Hirai (1969) made a similar test of Zen meditators in Japan. They took their EEG unit to a zendo and measured monks engaged in intensive meditation. That the Zen monks were trying to cultivate an attitude of mindfulness was the hypothesis the investigators sought to test. The Zen meditators were presented with a repetitious stimulus, a series of 40 tapping sounds. If their meditation had produced the ability to be mindful, then they should be fully responsive to the entire sequence of taps. If they were merely in a normal state of wakefulness, then their alpha rhythms should be broken by each tap (a normal orienting response) until about the tenth tap or so; beyond that point, they should show no blocking of the alpha rhythm, a sign that they had habituated to the stimulus.

Kasamatsu and Hirai report that most of the Zen meditators did habituate to the taps, indicating that they were not in an altered state. However, the three monks that were rated by their teacher as most advanced responded as strongly to the last tap as they did to the first tap—a pattern that signifies a state of mindful, ongoing alertness beyond the normal range of waking states.

Replication. The two studies described here are often cited but have never been successfully repeated. Both were done during the early days of EEG research without the aid of computer analysis or other current techniques. Each study should be replicated to establish whether these attentional training techniques can result in the altered states described in the classical literature. Such a replication would require a very careful choice of subjects and measures: The level of achievement required in the subjects is quite high—and rare. It would be easy to obtain a false negative because the wrong subjects were studied. The subjects must be actually practicing an attentional maneuver that should result in the hypothesized change. Many Zen meditators, for example, practice techniques other than mindfulness. The most likely candidates to replicate the mindfulness study would be found among advanced practitioners of Theravadan-style insight meditation (Brown, 1984). The most appropriate measure of brain activity for these studies would be the evoked potential, perhaps in tandem with the alpha-based measures used in the older studies. The evoked potential represents a powerful measure of the brain's central processes and might provide a more definitive replication.

A full EEG spectrum analysis would also be a helpful additional measure, particularly in tracing the cartography of subtly different altered states in meditation. Again, caution must be exercised in choosing subjects. Because the states to be assessed are themselves fragile and few practitioners are skilled enough to evoke them on demand, a comparison across subjects can only yield fruitful findings if the meditators are suitably adept.

Meditative Altered Traits and States. The goals of the various meditative paths, while couched in very different terms, share a common aim: the retooling of consciousness.

Although each tradition describes "those who have arrived" in its own language and in accordance with its own cosmology and belief system, there are marked overlaps. The personality traits described for the arahat in classical Buddhism serve as well as any to represent the ideal type of the "finished" being.

An exemplary study of meditators at various levels of accomplishment was performed by Brown and Engler (1980), who administered a battery of personality tests on accomplished Buddhist insight meditators in America and Asia. One finding from this study is particularly seminal. Meditators who underwent three months of intensive training in insight meditation were given Rorschach tests before and after their training. Independently, their teacher rated each on how well they had developed one-pointedness or mindfulness. The Rorschach responses of subjects who rated highest in each were compared. Those adept at one-pointedness gave sparse, unimaginative responses; those adept at mindfulness gave plentiful responses with rich associations. The pattern of Rorschach responses seems to reflect the consequences of meditative training; powerful one-pointedness means the meditator disregards the train of mental associations, while strong mindfulness means the meditator notes each and every element in his stream of consciousness. It is unclear from this study as to how long these traits of awareness would persist after the meditators returned to their normal lives.

Other studies have documented a range of lasting effects from meditation, although they do not address whether the long-term effects are by-products of meditation in general or specific to one attentional strategy. These trait effects include perceptual sharpening and decreased distractibility (Pelletier, 1974; Van Nuys, 1971), autonomic stability and quickened recovery from stress arousal (Orme-Johnson, 1973; Goleman and Schwartz, 1976), and lowered general anxiety level (Davidson, Goleman, and Schwartz, 1976).

The Abhidhamma proposes that meditation can produce certain lasting changes in personality. Recent empirical studies of personality in meditators bear on the major predicted change of a decrease in negative and increase in positive psychological states. For example, meditators, compared to nonmeditators, have been found to be significantly less anxious (Ferguson and Gowan, 1976; Goleman and Schwartz, 1976; Nidich et al., 1973), report fewer psychosomatic disorders, more positive moods, and are less neurotic on Eysenck's scale (Schwartz, 1973). Meditators also show an increased independence of situational cues, that is, an internal locus of control (Pelletier, 1974); are more spontaneous, have greater capacity for intimate contact, are more accepting of self, and have higher self-regard (Seeman et al., 1972); are better at empathizing with another person (Lesh, 1970; Leung, 1973); and show less fear of death (Garfield, 1974). Although these studies were not specifically designed to assess the Abhidhamma formulations of the impact of meditation on personality, their findings tend to bear out its major premise: that meditation reduces negative states while increasing positive ones.

The research literature suggests in a rough-and-ready fashion that there are both state and trait effects from meditative training. As with state effects, the trait effects found to date are in need of replication and extension. There are two general designs that might prove most useful in bringing out these long-term effects: baseline profiles and performance indices in response to challenge.

There is as yet no methodologically tight study of the long-term effects of meditation (Shapiro, 1980). Ideally, such a study would control for subjects' initial differences (such as in motivation), randomly assign them to treatments, and assess measures both pre- and post-treatment. A definitive study would take these factors into account and then measure its subjects on a range of dimensions relevant to meditation-induced changes. Standard personality batteries, behavioral measures, and, in particular, brain-based measures of attention are the primary candidates. Meditators' own reports and the classical literature as well as contemporary research findings should be consulted in forming specific hypotheses.

Many traits manifest only under specific conditions. For example, studies of hypertensives show that a blood pressure reading taken of a person at rest may be within the normal range, while a reading taken under stress will indicate hypertension. At rest, some special attributes of meditators may be latent, while stress or other conditions may evoke these attributes. A range of performance tests could assess such hidden capacities.

Whatever the specifics of design and measurement, the most fruitful research will be guided by the wisdom of Eastern psychologies. These psychologies can offer a theoretical perspective on the course of changes in meditation that can inform research. Few studies of meditation to date have been done within the context of an overarching theoretical point of view. Most studies have been piecemeal, some measuring brain waves, others looking at metabolic changes, still others assessing psychological effects. The reports from scientific laboratories read a bit like the tale of the six blind men and the elephant.

The Eastern psychologies, however, offer many theories and testable hypotheses on what meditation is and does. Refining these hypotheses would result in a Western understanding of meditation that is well-grounded in both theory and data. One excellent example of how this work might be pursued is Daniel Brown's (1984) research on perceptual changes in vipassana meditators.

There is a plentiful array of working hypotheses to be found in the Eastern psychologies. With a template such as this to guide it, meditation research can grow to be a valuable contribution to our understanding of human consciousness.

Meditation and Flow: Living in the Tao

The arahat, it is said, at all times and in every circumstance experiences an internal state of calm delight, is keenly attentive to all important aspects of the situation, and exhibits "skillful means" in response to the requirements of the moment. A similar state has been described in contemporary psychology by Csikzentmihalyi (1978), who has studied a broad range of intrinsically rewarding activities, all of which are marked by a similar experience, which he calls "flow."

The key elements of flow are: (a) the merging of action and awareness in sustained concentration on the task at hand, (b) the focusing of attention in a pure involvement without concern for outcome, (c) self-forgetfulness with heightened awareness of the activity, (d) skills adequate to meet the environmental demand, and (e) clarity regarding situational cues and appropriate response. Flow arises when there is an optimal fit between one's capability and the demands of the moment. The flow range is bordered on the one hand by anxiety-inducing situations where demand exceeds capability, and on the other hand by boredom where capability far exceeds demand.

In a related work Hartmann (1973) proposes a pattern of "inhibitory sharpening" in cortical arousal patterning, which represents optimal specificity of brain response to environmental demand. Focused attention entails clearly demarcated small areas of cortical excitation surrounded by areas of inhibition.

When blurring occurs in the brain's demarcation of excitation and inhibition, there is a "spillover" of arousal to brain areas irrelevant to the task at hand. This, proposes Hartmann, characterizes a less balanced, less delicately adjusted cortical functioning, as is found during tiredness. Such an excitation "spillover" may also occur in acute anxiety, and may account for the lessened ability to perceive and respond in anxiety states. Finely tuned cortical specificity, on the other hand, characterizes well-rested waking functioning, allowing flexibility in meeting environmental demands with skilled response. This should be one aspect of the neurophysiologic substrate of flow.

As I interpret the flow model in terms of neurophysiology, Hartmann's formulation points up a significant characteristic of flow: It requires both precision and fluidity in neurologic patterning, so that activation can change tailored to fluctuating situational requirements. The flow state is not a given pattern of ongoing arousal; it demands state-flexibility. The person who is chronically anxious, or habitually locked into *any* given configuration of arousal, is likely to confront more situations where his internal state is inappropriate for optimal fit with environmental demands—that is, non-flow. Changing circumstances require changing internal states.

There are two ways of increasing the likelihood of a flow experience: regulating environmental challenge to fit one's skills, as in games, or self-regulation of internal capacities to meet a greater variation in external demands. I propose that meditation may be a functional equivalent of the latter strategy, producing a change in internal state which could maximize possibilities for flow.

"Some people," notes Csikzentmihalyi, "enter flow simply by directing their awareness so as to limit the stimulus field in a way that allows the merging of action and awareness"—namely, attentional focus with the exclusion of distracting stimuli. This is identical to the basic skill practiced in meditation: it is the essential core of every meditative discipline (though techniques may vary according to the degree of attentional effort expended).

A constellation of findings on the enduring effects of meditation suggests a spectrum of changes, which include perceptual sharpening and increased ability to attend to a target stimulus while ignoring irrelevant stimuli; increased cortical specificity—that is, arousal of the cortical area appropriate to a given task with relative inhibition of irrelevant cortical zones, a pattern underlying skilled response; increased situation-specific cortical arousability with limbic inhibition; autonomic stability and lowering of anxiety level; and equanimity and evenness in responding to emotionally loaded and threatening stimuli.

To the extent that these diverse findings are true for any individual meditator, these traits should operate so as to lower the threshold for entering flow by bringing into its domain those instances where flow would otherwise have been excluded by misperception, distractability, arousal states unsuited to specific requirements, or functioning impaired by anxiety. As the range of flow and its sense of the intrinsic rewards of activity expands, there would be a concomitant shrinkage in the domains both of anxiety-inducing and boring situations in daily life. Indeed the fitting of one's internal state to the demands of specific action, as in flow, has been an ideal of many Asian systems for self-development. In the words of the Zen master Unmon: "If you walk, just walk. If you sit, just sit. But whatever you do, don't wobble."

The phenomenology of flow shares many attributes of the meditation adept's mental state as described in Abhidhamma: clarity of perception, alertness, equanimity; and pliancy, efficiency, and skill in action. To the degree that the lasting effects of meditation approach this ideal, the flow state can be seen as one benefit of meditation.

In this sense the goal of meditation training coincides in part with the qualities of skilled behavior and, more generally, with flow: action unimpeded by anxiety, clarity of perception, and accuracy of response, pleasure in action for its own sake. The nature of this experience is aptly capsulized in Merton's translation of a poem by the Taoist master Chuang Tzu:

> Ch'ui the draftsman
> Could draw more perfect circles freehand
> Than with a compass.
>
> His fingers brought forth
> Spontaneous forms from nowhere. His mind
> Was meanwhile free and without concern.
>
> No drives, no compulsions,
> No needs, no attractions:
> Then your affairs
> Are under control.
> You are a free man.

How to Meditate

For the reader who would like to try meditating, here are some simple practices. You can try them all, but if you are going to continue to meditate, it is best to stick with the one you find most to your liking.

Find a comfortable, straight-back chair in a quiet room where you will not be disturbed. Sit up straight but relaxed. Keep your head, neck, and spine aligned, as though a large helium balloon was lifting your head up. Keeping your head upright will help your mind stay more alert—and alertness is essential in meditation.

Close your eyes and keep them closed until the session has ended. It's best to sit for at least 15 minutes at a time, preferably longer—20 or 30 minutes or even an hour if possible. You should decide how long you plan to sit be fore you begin. That way you won't yield so easily to the temptation to get up and do something "urgent" or "more useful." Urges to stop meditating will come and go, and you should resist them. Set a timer or peek at your watch from time to time to see if the session is over.

Meditation on the Breath. One of the simplest practices is meditation on the breath. This practice cultivates both concentration and mindfulness. Although it was the method that reportedly brought the Buddha to enlightenment, it also has found a more mundane use in psychotherapy and behavioral medicines as a technique for becoming deeply relaxed.

To begin, bring your awareness to your breath, noticing each inhalation and exhalation. You can watch the breath either by feeling the sensations at the nostrils or by noting the rise and fall of your belly as you breathe.

Try to be aware of each breath for its full duration: the entire in-breath, the entire out-breath. Do not try to control your breath—just watch it. If your breathing gets more shallow, let it be shallow. If it gets faster or slower, let it. The breath regulates itself. While you meditate, your job is simply to be aware of it.

Whenever you notice that your mind has wandered, gently bring it back to your breath. During meditation, your contract with yourself is that everything other than your breath—thoughts, plans, memories, sounds, sensations—are distractions. Let go of your other thoughts. Whatever comes into your mind besides your breath is, for now, a distraction.

If you have trouble keeping your mind on your breath, you can help maintain your focus by repeating a word with each inhalation and exhalation. If you are watching your breath at the nostril, think "in" with each inhalation, "out" with each exhalation. If you are watching the rise and fall of your belly, think "rising" with each inhalation, "falling" with each exhalation. Be sure to stay in touch with the actual experience of breathing, not merely the repetition of the words.

Mantra.   Some of the most widely used concentrative meditations employ mantras as the objects of focus. These techniques, as we have seen, are found in virtually every major spiritual tradition, from Christianity, Judaism, and Islam to Buddhism and Hinduism. In modern times, the technique has been adapted as the "relaxation response" to help people enter a relaxed state.

Pick a simple word or sound that has a positive meaning to you. Many people select a phrase that has spiritual symbolism for them, such as "adonai," "kyrie eleison," or "one." In Hinduism, names of God such as "Ram" are common; in Tibetan Buddhism, the mantra "Om Mane Padme Hum" is often used.

Once you decide what mantra you will use, the directions are similar to those for the breath meditation. Sit quietly and repeat your mantra mentally to yourself without making any actual sound. Whenever your mind wanders, bring it back to the mantra. Let go of all other thoughts, letting the mantra fill your consciousness.

Mindful Breathing. To cultivate mindfulness, start with the simple meditation on the breath described above. Once you have gained a fairly firm hold on meditating on the breath, you can expand the practice into a more general mindfulness—a meditation on the mind itself. In mindfulness meditation, everything that goes on in your mind becomes the object of meditation.

Again, use the breath as your basic object of meditation. But now, whenever your mind wanders, be aware of the nature of its wandering. In other words, use your distractions as objects of meditation.

For example, if your mind wanders to a sound you hear, label that distraction "hearing." If your mind wanders to a thought, call it "thinking"; if to a memory, label it "remembering"; if to a sensation in your body, call it "feeling." Each time you have labeled the distraction, bring your mind back to the breath once again.

Mindful Eating. With mindfulness, any activity can be meditative if you pay full and careful attention to what you are doing. Take, for instance, eating. The method in mindful eating is to pay careful and full attention to every aspect of the experience.

Begin by sitting still and bringing your attention to your breath, watching the in- and out-breath. When you feel collected and still, begin to eat.

It helps to eat very slowly, breaking down each movement so that you can attend to each nuance of sensation, sound, taste, and movement. For example, as you reach for a bite of food, do it at a speed in which you can note the stretch and tension of the muscles in your arm and hand and the feel of the food or fork against your skin. Avoid the tendency to go on "automatic," to reach for the next bite before you finish with the current one.

Let's say you're going to eat almonds. Pick up one and hold it between your fingers. Feel the texture of its skin against your fingertips and the shape and pressure while holding it. Look at it: Notice its color and outline and the grooves along its sides.

Slowly raise the almond to your mouth. Notice the moment you can first smell it. If you're attentive, you may notice you've started salivating before the almond reaches your mouth. Be aware of the first brush of the almond on your lips.

Next, put it in your mouth and start chewing slowly and deliberately. Notice the feel of your teeth biting through the almond and the work of your tongue as it moves the chunks of almond inside your mouth. Note the nut's taste. Listen to the sounds of chewing. Tune in to the sensations created by every bite.

Notice how the chewed almond bits mix with saliva as you swallow. Be sure to chew all the bits completely and to swallow them before you take another almond. Continue eating each remaining almond with the same careful deliberateness. Stay calm and focused throughout.

Mindful Walking. Take your shoes off. Stand in one place and feel the sensations in your feet as they touch the ground. Stay with whatever you feel at each moment. As you are about to take a step forward, notice your mental intention to step forward. Slowly lift your foot, feeling every sensation—lightness, suspension, tension, motion—whatever feelings are present.

It's best to start at a slow pace so you can pay attention to the sensations. Eventually, you'll be able to go faster and yet maintain awareness. Move your foot forward, place it on the ground again, and shift your weight onto it. All the time, be aware of the sensations in this movement. When thoughts arise, don't be concerned with their content. Bring your mind back to your foot feelings and stay with this simple experience of walking. Continue to do this as long as you like—five minutes to half an hour or longer.

At first, to keep your mind focused, it helps to label the action. For example, you can say silently, "Up—forward—down," noticing the feeling of weight as it shifts from one foot to the other. Later you can simplify the process by eliminating the words. Just concentrate on the sensation.

To observe the process of mind in greater detail, note the intention that precedes each motion, as well as the sensations themselves. Thus: *intending* to lift, lifting; *intending* to move forward, moving forward; *intending* to place, placing; *intending* to shift, shifting.

Finally, you can develop a direct perception of the entire routine—intent, movement, sensations—without labeling any of it.

BIBLIOGRAPHY

ABU AL-NAJIB. *A Sufi Rule for Novices.* Translated by M. Milson. Cambridge, Mass.: Harvard University Press, 1975.

ALEXANDER, F. *The Scope of Psychoanalysis.* New York: Basic Books, 1941.

ALLPORT, GORDON. *The Person in Psychology.* Boston: Beacon, 1968.

AMMA. *Dhyan-yoga and Kundalini Yoga.* Ganeshpuri, India: Shree Gurudev Ashram, 1969.

ANAND, B. K.; CHINA, G. S.; and SINGH, B. "Some Aspects of EEG Studies in Yogis." *EEG and Clinical Neurophysiology,* 13(1961):452–456.

ANANDA MAYEE MA. *Matri Vani.* Edited by Gurupriya Devi. Varanasi, India: Shree Anandashram, 1972.

ARBERRY, A. J. *Sufism: An Account of the Mystics of Islam.* London: Allen & Unwin, 1972.

ASSAGIOLI, A. *Psychosynthesis.* New York: Viking, 1971.

BABBITT, I., trans. *The Dhammapada.* New York: New Directions, 1965.

BECKER, E. *Angel in Armor.* New York: Free Press, 1969.

BENNETT, J. G. *Gurdjieff: Making a New World.* London: Turnstone Books, 1973.

BENSON, HERBERT. *The Relaxation Response.* New York: William Morrow, 1975.

BERGER, P. L., and LUCKMANN, T. *The Social Construction of Reality.* New York: Doubleday, 1967.

BHARATI, AGEHANANDA. *The Tantric Tradition.* Garden City, N.Y.: Anchor Books, Doubleday, 1970.

BHIKKU SOMA. *The Way of Mindfulness.* Colombo, Ceylon: Vajirama, 1949.

BLOFELD, J. *The Zen Teaching of Hui Hai.* London: Rider, 1962.

BOSS, MEDARD. *A Psychiatrist Discovers India.* London: Oswald Wolff, 1965.

BROWN, DANIEL P. "A Model for the Levels of Concentrative Meditation." *International Journal of Clinical and Experimental Hypnosis,* 25 (1977):236–273.

BROWN, DANIEL P., and ENGLER, JACK. "The Stages of Mindfulness Meditation: A Validation Study." *Journal of Transpersonal Psychology,* 12 (1980):143–192.

BROWN, D. P.; FORTE, M.; and DYSART, M. "Differences in Visual Sensitivity Among Mindfulness Meditators and Non-Meditators." *Perceptual and Motor Skills,* 58 (1984):227–233.

BUCKE, R. M. *Cosmic Consciousness.* New York: Dutton, 1969.

BUDDHAGHOSA. *Visuddhimagga: The Path of Purification.* Translated by B. Nyanamoli. Berkeley: Shambhala, 1976.

BUTLER, D. C. *Western Mysticism.* New York: Harper, 1966.

CHADWICK, A. W. *A Sadhu's Reminiscences of Ramana Maharshi.* Tiruvannamalai, India: Sri Ramanasram, 1966.

CHANG, G. C. C. *The Hundred Thousand Songs of Milarepa.* New York: Harper Colophon Books, 1970.

CHOGYAM TRUNGPA. *Cutting Through Spiritual Materialism.* Berkeley: Shambhala, 1975.

————. *The Myth of Freedom.* Berkeley: Shambhala, 1976.

COHEN, ALAN, et al. "Psychophysiology of Relaxation-Associated Panic Attacks." *Journal of Abnormal Psychology,* 94(1985):96–100.

COLEMAN, J. E. *The Quiet Mind.* London: Rider & Co., 1971.

CONZE, E. *Buddhist Meditation.* London: Allen & Unwin, 1956.

CSIKZENTMIHALYI, M. *Between Boredom and Anxiety.* San Francisco: Josey-Bass, 1978.

DALAI LAMA, THE FOURTEENTH. *An Introduction to Buddhism.* New Delhi, India: Tibet House, 1965.

DAVIDSON, J. M. "The Physiology of Meditation and Mystical States of Consciousness." *Perspectives in Biology and Medicine,* 19 (1976):345–379.

DAVIDSON, R. J.; GOLEMAN, D.; and SCHWARTZ, G. E. "Attentional and Affective Concomitants of Meditation: A Cross-Sectional Study." *Journal of Abnormal Psychology,* 85(1976):235–238.

DOGEN. *A Primer of Soto Zen.* Honolulu: University of Hawaii Press, 1971.

DOYLE, L. J., trans. *St. Benedict's Rule for Monasteries.* Collegeville, Minn.: The Liturgical Press, 1948.

ELIADE, M. *Yoga: Immortality and Freedom.* Princeton: Princeton University Press, 1970.

ERIKSON, ERIK. *Childhood and Society.* New York: Norton, 1963.

EVANS-WENTZ, W. Y. *Tibetan Yoga and Secret Doctrines.* London: Oxford University Press, 1968.

————. *The Tibetan Book of the Dead.* New York: Oxford University Press, 1969.

————. *The Tibetan Book of the Great Liberation.* London: Oxford University Press, 1969.

FERGUSON, P., and GOWAN, J. "TM: Some Preliminary Findings." *Journal of Humanistic Psychology,* 16(1976):51–60.

FRENCH, R. M., trans. *The Way of the Pilgrim.* New York: Seabury Press, 1970.

GARFIELD, C. "Consciousness Alteration and Fear of Death." *Journal of Transpersonal Psychology,* 7(1974):147–175.

GOFFMAN, E. *Asylums.* New York: Doubleday, 1962.

GOLEMAN, D., and SCHWARTZ, G. E. "Meditation As an Intervention in Stress Reactivity." *Journal of Clinical and Consulting Psychology,* 44(1976):456–466.

GOVINDA, LAMA ANAGARIKA. *The Psychological Attitude of Early Buddhist Philosophy.* London: Rider, 1969.

GUENTHER, H. V. *Philosophy and Psychology in the Abhidhamma.* Berkeley: Shambhala, 1976.

GUENTHER, H. V., and CHOGYAM TRUNGPA. *The Dawn of Tantra.* Berkeley: Shambhala, 1975.

GURDJIEFF, G. I. *The Herald of Coming Good.* New York: Samuel Weiser, 1971.

HALEVI, Z'EV BEN SHIMON. *The Way of Kabbalah.* New York: Samuel Weiser, 1976.

HARTMANN, E. *The Functions of Sleep.* New Haven: Yale University Press, 1973.

HESSE, H. *Siddhartha.* New York: Bantam, 1970.

————. *Journey to the East.* New York: Bantam, 1971.

JAMES, W. *The Principles of Psychology.* 1910. Reprint. New York: Dover, 1950.

————. *The Varieties of Religious Experience.* New York: Crowell-Collier, 1961.

JOHANSSON, R. E. A. *The Psychology of Nirvana.* New York: Anchor, 1970.

JUNG, C. G. "Psychology and Religion: West and East." In *Collected Works,* vol. 11. Princeton: Princeton University Press, 1958.

————. "Psychology and Alchemy." In *Collected Works,* vol. 12. Princeton: Princeton University Press, 1968.

KABAT-ZINN, JON, et al. "The Clinical Use of Mindfulness Meditation for the Self-Regulation of Chronic Pain." *Journal of Behavioral Medicine,* 8(1985):163–189.

KABIR. *Poems of Kabir.* Translated by R. Tagore. Calcutta: Macmillan, 1970.

KADLOUBOVSKY, E., and PALMER, G. E. H. *Early Fathers from the Philokalia.* London: Faber & Faber, 1969.

————. *Writings from the Philokalia on Prayer of the Heart.* London: Faber & Faber, 1971.

KALU RIMPOCHE. *The Foundation of Buddhist Meditation.* Dharamsala, India: Library of Tibetan Works and Archives, 1974.

KAPLEAU, P. *The Three Pillars of Zen.* Boston: Beacon Press, 1967.

KASAMATSU, A., and HIRAI, T. "An EEG Study on the Zen Meditation." In *Altered States of Consciousness,* edited by C. Tart. New York: Wiley, 1969.

KASHYAP, J. *The Abhidhamma Philosophy.* Vol 1. Nalanda, India: Buddha Vihara, 1954.

KATZ, R. "Education for Transcendence: Lessons from the !Kung Zhũ/twãsi." *Journal of Transpersonal Psychology,* 5, 2(1973):136–155.

KIECOLT-GLASER, JANICE K., et al. "Psychosocial Enhancement of Immunocompetence in a Geriatric Population." *Health Psychology,* 4, 1(1985):25–41.

————. "Modulation of Cellular Immunity in Medical Students." *Journal of Behavioral Medicine,* May 1986.

KRISHNAMURTI, J. *Commentaries on Living.* Edited by D. Rajagopal. 3d series. London: Victor Gollancz, 1962.

LAO TZU. *Tao Te Ching.* Translated by D. C. Lau. Baltimore: Penguin, 1963.

LEDI SAYADAW. *Gospel of Sri Ramakrishna.* Mylapore, India: Sri Ramakrishna Math, 1928.

————. *The Manuals of Buddhism.* Rangoon, Burma: Union Buddha Sasana Council, 1965.

LEHRER, PAUL, and HOCHRON, STUART. "Relaxation Decreases Asthma in Asthmatic Subjects With Large-Airway Constriction." *Journal of Psychosomatic Research,* February 1986.

LESH, T. V. "Zen Meditation and the Development of Empathy in Counselors." *Journal of Humanistic Psychology,* 10(1970):39–54.

LEUNG, P. "Comparative Effects of Training in External and Internal Concentration on Two Counseling Behaviors." *Journal of Counseling Psychology,* 20(1973):227–234.

M. *The Gospel of Sri Ramakrishna.* New York: Rama Vivekananda Center, 1952.

MAHARISHI MAHESH YOGI. *The Science of Being and the Art of Living.* Los Angeles: SRM Publications, 1966.

————. *On the Bhagavad Gita.* Baltimore: Penguin, 1969.

MAHASI SAYADAW. *The Process of Insight.* Translated by Nyanaponika Thera. Kandy, Ceylon: The Forest Hermitage, 1965.

————. *Buddhist Meditation and Its Forty Subjects.* Buddha-gaya, India: International Meditation Center, 1970.

MAHATHERA, P. V. *Buddhist Meditation in Theory and Practice.* Colombo, Ceylon: Gunaseca, 1962.

MARMION, REV. D. COLUMBA. *Christ the Ideal of the Monk.* St. Louis: Herder, 1926.

MASLOW, A. *Religions, Values, and Peak-experiences.* New York: Harper & Row, 1964.

————. "Theory Z." *Journal of Transpersonal Psychology,* 2, 1(1970):31–47.

————. *The Farther Reaches of Human Nature.* New York: Viking Press, 1971.

MEHER BABA. *Discourses I, II, III.* San Francisco: Sufism Reoriented, 1967.

MERTON, T. *The Wisdom of the Desert.* New York: New Directions, 1960.

————. *The Way of Chuang Tzu.* London: Allen & Unwin, 1965.

MIURA, I., and SASAKI, R. F. *The Zen Koan.* New York: Harcourt, Brace & World, 1965.

MUKTANANDA PARAMAHANSA, SWAMI. *Soham-japa.* New Delhi, India: Siddha Yoga Dham, 1969.

————. *Gurukripa.* Ganeshpuri, India: Shree Gurudev Ashram, 1970.

————. *Guruvani Magazine.* Ganeshpuri, India: Shree Gurudev Ashram, 1971.

————. *Guru.* New York: Harper & Row, 1972.

NANAMOLI THERA. *Mindfulness of Breathing.* Kandy, Ceylon: Buddhist Publication Society, 1964.

————. *Visuddhimagga: The Path of Purification.* Berkeley: Shambhala, 1976.

NARADA, M. *A Manual of Abhidhamma.* Kandy, Sri Lanka: Buddhist Publication Society, 1968.

NARADA THERA. *A Manual of Abhidhamma, I & II.* Colombo, Ceylon: Vajirarama, 1956.

NICHOLSON, R. A. *Studies in Islamic Mysticism.* Cambridge: Cambridge University Press, 1929.

NIDICH, S.; SEEMAN, W.; and DRESKIN, T. "Influence of Transcendental Meditation: A Replication." *Journal of Counseling Psychology,* 20(1973):565–566.

NYANAPONIKA, T., trans. *Anguttara nikaya.* Kandy, Sri Lanka: Buddhist Publication Society, 1975.

NYANAPONIKA THERA. *Abhidhamma Studies.* Colombo, Ceylon: Frewin, 1949.

————. *The Heart of Buddhist Meditation.* London: Rider, 1962.

————. *The Power of Mindfulness.* Kandy, Ceylon: Buddhist Publication Society, 1968.

————. *Pathways of Buddhist Thought.* London: George Allen and Unwin, 1971.

NYANATILOKA MAHATHERA. *The Word of the Buddha.* Colombo, Ceylon: Buddha Publishing Committee, 1952a.

————. *Path to Deliverance.* Colombo, Ceylon: Buddha Sahitya Sabha, 1952b.

————. *Buddhist Dictionary: Manual of Buddhist Terms and Doctrines.* Colombo, Ceylon: Frewin & Co., 1972.

ORME-JOHNSON, D. W. "Autonomic Stability and Transcendental Meditation." *Psychosomatic Medicine,* 35, 4(1973):341–349.

ORNISH, DEAN, et al. "Effects of Stress Management Training and Dietary Changes in Treating Ischemic Heart Disease." *Journal of the American Medical Association,* 247(1983):54–59.

OUSPENSKY, P. D. *The Fourth Way.* New York: Vintage, 1971.

PATEL, CHANDRA, et al. "Trial of Relaxation in Reducing Coronary Risk: Four-Year Follow-Up." *British Medical Journal,* 290 (1985):1103–1106.

PELLETIER, K. "Influence of TM Upon Autokinetic Perception." *Perceptual and Motor Skills,* 30(1974):1031–1034.

PODDAR, H. P. *The Divine Name and Its Practice.* Gorakhpur, India: Gita Press, 1965.

PRABHAVANANDA, SWAMI, and ISHERWOOD, C. *How to Know God: Yoga Aphorisms of Patanjali.* New York: Signet, 1969.

RAMANA MAHARSHI. *Maharshi's Gospel, I & II.* Tiruvannamalai, India: Sri Ramanasram, 1962.

RAMANUJAN, C. K. *Speaking of Shiva.* Baltimore: Penguin, 1973.

RICE, C. *The Persian Sufis.* London: Allen & Unwin, 1964.

RUDI. *Spiritual Cannibalism.* New York: Quick Fox, 1973.

ST. JOHN OF THE CROSS. *Ascent of Mount Carmel.* Translated by E. Allison Peers. Garden City, N.Y.: Image Books, 1958.

SAMYUTTA-NIKAYA. *Scripture.* London: Pali Text Society, 1972.

SARADANANDA, SWAMI. *Ramakrishna the Great Master.* Mylapore, India: Sri Ramakrishna Math, 1963.

SATPREM. *Sri Aurobindo: The Adventure of Consciousness.* Translated by Tehmi. Pondicherry, India: Sri Aurobindo Society, 1970.

SCHOLEM, G. *Kabbalah.* New York: Quadrangle/The New York Times Book Co., 1974.

SCHUMAN, MARJORIE. "The Psychophysiological Model of Meditation and Altered States of Consciousness: A Critical Review." In *The Psychobiology of Consciousness,* edited by J. M. Davidson and R. J. Davidson. New York: Plenum, 1980.

SCHWARTZ, G. E. "Pros and Cons of Meditation: Current Findings on Physiology and Anxiety, Self-Control, Drug Abuse, and Creativity." Paper presented at American Psychological Association meeting, Montreal, September 1973.

SEEMAN, W.; NIDCH, S.; and BANTA, T. "A Study of the Influence of Transcendental Meditation on a Measure of Self-Actualization." *Journal of Counseling Psychology,* 19(1972):184–187.

SELYE, HANS. *The Stress of Life.* New York: McGraw-Hill, 1978.

SHAH, I. *Wisdom of the Idiots.* New York: Dutton, 1971.

———. *The Sufis.* New York: Doubleday, 1972.

SHAPIRO, DEANE. *Meditation: A Scientific and Personal Exploration.* New York: Aldine, 1980.

SHAPIRO, D., and WALSH, R. *Meditation: Classical and Contemporary Views.* New York: Aldine, 1984.

SRIMAD BHAGAVATAM. Gorakhpur, India: Gita Press, 1969.

STEWART, K. "Dream Theory in Malaya." In *Altered States of Consciousness,* edited by C. Tart. New York: Wiley, 1969.

SURWIT, R., and FEINGLOS, M. "Effects of Relaxation on Glucose Tolerance." *Diabetes Care,* 6(1983).

SUTICH, A. "Statement of Purpose." *Journal of Transpersonal Psychology,* 1(1969):1.

SUZUKI, D. T. *The Zen Doctrine of No-Mind.* London: Rider, 1949.

———. *Essays in Zen Buddhism.* 2d series. London: Rider, 1958.

———. *The Field of Zen.* New York: Harper & Row, 1970.

———. *An Introduction to Zen Buddhism.* New York: Causeway, 1974.

TART, C. "Scientific Foundations for the Study of Altered States of Consciousness." *Journal of Transpersonal Psychology,* 3(1971):93–124.

———. *Transpersonal Psychologies.* New York: Harper & Row, 1976.

———, ed. *Altered States of Consciousness.* New York: Wiley, 1969.

VAJIRANANA, P. *Buddhist Meditation in Theory and Practice.* Colombo, Sri Lanka: Gunasena, 1962.

VAN AUNG, Z., trans. *Compendium of Philosophy.* London: Pali Text Society, 1972.

VAN NUYS, D. "A Novel Technique for Studying Attention During Meditation." *Journal of Transpersonal* Psychology, 3, 3(1971):125–134.

VIVEKANANDA, SWAMI. *Bhakti-yoga.* Calcutta: Advaita Ashrama, 1964.

———. *Raja-yoga.* Calcutta: Advaita Ashrama, 1970.

VYAS DEV, SWAMI. *First Steps to Higher Yoga.* Gangotri, India: Yoga Niketan Trust, 1970.

WADDELL, E. *The Desert Fathers.* Ann Arbor, Mich.: University of Michigan Press, 1957.

WALKER, K. *A Study of Gurdjieff's Teaching.* London: Jonathan Cape, 1969.

WATSON, J. B. "Psychology as a Behaviorist Views It." *Psychology Review,* 20(1913):158–177.

WATTS, A. *Psychotherapy East and West.* New York: Pantheon, 1961.

WEI WU WEI. *Posthumous Pieces.* Hong Kong: Hong Kong University Press, 1968.

WILBER, K.; ENGLER, J.; and BROWN, D. P. *Transformations of Consciousness.* Boston and London: New Science Library, 1986.

WILHELM, R., trans. *The Secret of the Golden Flower.* London: Routledge and Kegan Paul, 1969.

SUGGESTED READINGS

On Meditation Practice

DASS, RAM. *Journey of Awakening.* New York: Bantam Books, 1978.
FIELDS, RICK, et al. *Chop Wood, Carry Water.* Los Angeles: Jeremy P. Tarcher, 1984.
GOLDSTEIN, JOSEPH. *The Experience of Insight.* Boston: Shambhala, 1976.
KORNFIELD, JACK, and GOLDSTEIN, JOSEPH. *Seeking the Heart of Wisdom.* Boston: Shambhala, 1987.
LESHAN, LARRY. *How to Meditate.* New York: Bantam Books, 1975.
LEVINE, STEPHEN. *A Gradual Awakening.* New York: Doubleday, 1979.
ROSHI, SUSUKI. *Zen Mind, Beginner's Mind.* New York: Weatherhill, 1970.

On Eastern Psychologies, Meditation and Psychotherapy, and Meditation and Health

BENSON, HERBERT. *The Relaxation Response.* New York: William Morrow, 1975.
BORYSENKO, JOAN. *Minding the Body, Mending the Mind.* Reading, Mass.: Addison-Wesley, 1987.
SHAPIRO, DEANE, and WALSH, ROGER. *Meditation: Classic and Contemporary Perspectives.* Hawthorne, N.Y.: De Gruyter Aldine, 1984.

TART, CHARLES, ed. *Transpersonal Psychologies.* New York: Harper & Row, 1976.

WALSH, ROGER, and SHAPIRO, DEANE, eds. *Beyond Health and Normality.* New York: Van Nostrand Reinhold, 1983.

WILBER, KEN; ENGLER, JACK; and BROWN, DANIEL. *Transformations of Consciousness.* Boston and London: New Science Library, 1986.

INDEX

Abba Dorotheus, St., 54
Abdul-Hamid, 62
Abhidhamma, 1, 173
  on categories of mental
    factors, 119–127, 132–133
  development of, 115–116
  flow and, 184
  on mental health through
    meditation, 133–137
  mind-body interconnectedness
    in, 125
  on motivation, 127–128
  on *nirvana,* 136–137
  on personality, 127, 179
  psychological concepts of,
    114–139
  on reorganization of
    consciousness, 134–135
  on self, 117–118
  Western psychologists and,
    146
Abhidharma. See Abhidhamma
Absorption. *See* Jhanas
Abu al-Najib, 62
Abulafia, Abraham, 51
Abu Said of Mineh, 61

Access concentration, 11, 12, 21,
    68, 74
Adler, Alfred, 158
Advait Hinduism, 45, 66–67,
    108
Agitation *(uddhacca),* 122–123,
    131
Akiba, Rabbi, 51
Alexander, F., 148, 150
Al-Ghazali, 61
Al-Junaid of Baghdad, 62
Allport, Gordon, 147, 158
Al-Muridin, 63, 64–65
Alpha rhythm, 176
Al-Qushari, 60
Altered states of consciousness,
    110–113, 177–181
  versus altered traits of
    consciousness, 175
  Asian vocabularies for, 142,
    144
  cultural values and, 143–145
  frequency of experiences of,
    153
  Freud on, 140–141
  "technologies" for, 144, 145

"Altruistic joy" *(mudita),* 131
Amma, 81
Anagami (once returner), 33
Anand, B. K., 176
Ananda Mayee Ma, 42, 47
Anatta (realization of
    non-existence), 24, 32, 35
Anquttara nikaya, 122
Anicca. See Impermanence
Antony, St., 151
Anusayas, 132
Anxiety, 123, 131, 164, 168,
    179, 182, 183
Apperception *(phassa),* 121
Arahant. See Arahat
Arahat (awakened being),
    33–36, 83, 137–139, 147,
    178, 181
Arberry, A. J., 61
Asana (development of erect
    posture), 73, 78, 80
Ascetic practices, 6
Ashtanga yoga, 71–76
    final step in, 75–76
    first four limbs, 73–74
    second four limbs, 74–76
Assagioli, Alberto, 157
Asubhas, as meditation subjects,
    7
Atta (self), 117
Attention, spontaneous
    (manasikara), 121
Attention retraining, 11,
    110–111
    comparison of systems for
        means of, 104–107
    concentration and, 174
    entering flow and, 183
    James and, 145
    meditation and, 135–136,
        166–168, 169
Augustine, St., 57–58
Aurobindo, Sri, 109

Autogenic training, 169
Avarice *(macchariya),* 123, 125
Aversion *(dosa),* 123, 124, 125,
    131
Awakened being. *See Arahat*
Awakened states, 95–96,
    111–113.
    names for, 113. *See also
        specific names of such states,
        e.g.,* Bodhisattva
Azriel of Gerona, 51

Baba, Meher, 76
Baqa (life in Him), 62
"Bare attention," 89
"Bare insight," 21–22
Becker, E., 147–148
Behavior. *See also* Personality
    focusing on, 95
    influence of mental states on,
        127–131
    moral nature of, 120
    social, and purity, 3
Behaviorist psychology, 146
Benedict, St., 58
Bennett, J. G., 96–97
Benson, Herbert, 165, 169, 170
Berger, P. L., 108
Besant, Annie, 97
Beta-blockers, 170
Bhakti, 41–48, 53, 71–72
Bhakti Suttras, 44
Bharati, Agehananda, 79
Bhava (continuity of
    consciousness over time),
    117–118
Biofeedback, 169
Bishi al-Hafi, 59
Bodhisattva, 82, 86, 97
Body, 22, 125. *See also* Brain;
    Metabolism
Boss, Medard, 156–157
Brahma, union with, 66

Brain activity, 176–177
  Gurdjieffian versus
    Transcendental Meditation
    techniques and, 166–168
  meditation and, 165–168, 183
  research, 180
  spillover and, 182
Breathing, 17
  gearing recitation to, 42
  meditation on, 85–87
  Sufism on, 62
Brown, Daniel P., 149, 162,
    178, 181
Buber, Martin, 156
Bucke, R. M., 152, 160
Buddha, 5, 6, 9, 83, 115, 118,
    120, 122, 138, 173
Buddhaghosa, 1, 128
Buddhism. *See* Theravadan
    Buddhist meditation
    methods; Tibetan
    Buddhism; Zen
Buddhist psychology, 115. *See
  also Abhidhamma*
  levels of *jhana,* 144
  mental factors in, 119
  of personality, 116–119
  psychoanalysis and, 149–150
  of self, 122, 147
"Buddhist Training as an
    Artificial Catatonia"
    (Alexander), 148
Bushmen, 144
Butler, D. C., 58

Cardiovascular system, 170
"Cave of Satan," 90
Chadwick, A. W., 108
Chaitanya, Sri, 41
Chakras (physical centers), 77,
    81
Ch'an meditation school of
    China, 87

Chang, G. C. C., 86
Chanting and singing *(kirtan),*
    41, 80
Character, 128. *See also*
    Personality
Character armor, 147
Chogyam Trungpa, 84, 85–86
"Choiceless awareness," 98–101,
    105
Cholesterol levels, 170
Christian Hesychasm. *See*
    Hesychasm
Chuang Tzu, 92, 184
Civilization and Its Discontents
    (Freud), 140
Clairvoyance, 74, 138
Clarity, 123
Cohen, Alan, 171
Compassion, 34, 138
Composure *(passadhi),* 124–125,
    138
Concentration, path of
    (samadhi), 10–19, 105, 107,
    175, 176
  altered states and, 110
  Bhakti and, 44–45
  distractions and, 10–11
  entering, 7–9
  entering, preliminary stages,
    10–11
  goal of, 7
  jhanic levels, 13–19
  Krishnamurti on, 98
  landmarks on, 15
  maithuna and, 79
  maintaining, 135–136
  meditation subjects, 7–8
  mindfulness and, 21–22
  muscle control and, 167–168
  meditation subjects and, 12
  one-pointedness and, 174
  path to insight and, 3, 37
  purity and, 3, 7

Concentration *(continued)*
Tibetan Buddhism and, 83, 84
on verge of absorption, 11–12
visions and, 12–13
yoga and, 72–73, 74–76, 78
Zen and, 88–90
"Concentration games," 20
Conditioned reaction *(vedana)*, 121
Confessions (St. Augustine), 57
Confidence *(saddha)*, 124
Consciousness. *See also* Altered states of consciousness
altered traits of, 175
basic framework of, 121
Introspectionists on, 146
psychotherapy and, 173–174
reorganization of, 134–135
research studies, 175–181
transformation of, 137, 139, 150
Contemplation, St. Augustine on, 57–58
Contraction *(thina)*, 123
Control, 133, 179
"Cosmic consciousness," 68–70, 112
Csikzentmihalyi, M., 181, 183
Culture, 142–145

Daat (knowledge), 51–52, 107
Daigi (fixation), 88
Dalai Lama, 82, 84
Dance, 11, 144, 166–167
Darshan (visiting of saints), 42
Davidson, J. M., 175
Davidson, R. J., 179
Delusion *(moha)*, 121, 123, 127, 129, 130
DeMartino, Richard, 156
Desensitization, 123, 172–173

Desert Fathers. *See* Monks: Christian
Detachment, 26, 117
Devekut, 52
Devotional object *(ishta),* 41, 42, 43–44
Dhammapada, 120
Dharana (sixth limb of ashtanga yoga), 74
Dharma, 83
Dhyana (seventh limb of ashtanga yoga), 74
Diabetes, 171
"Directions to Hesychasts," 56
Discipline, codes of, 3
Discretion *(ottappa),* 124
Distractions, 10–11
Dogen, 87
Doyle, L. J., 58
Dreams, 34, 138, 144
Drugs, 153
Dukkha, 26, 32, 35

Eastern psychology, 114–116, 141–161. *See also* *Abhidhamma;* Buddhist psychology
alteration of consciousness and, 145
dissemination of, 150–162
durability of, 150
psychotherapy and, 173–174
research and, 180–181
Western psychology and, 139–162
Eating, and mindfulness, 187–188
Eckhardt, Meister, 151
EEG research, 176–177
Ego. *See* Self
Egoism *(mana),* 122, 124, 127–128. *See also* Self
Eliade, M., 76, 77, 79

Emerson, Ralph Waldo, 151
Engler, Jack, 162, 178
Environment, 182–183
Envy *(issa)*, 123, 124, 125
Epstein, Mark, 162
Equanimity, 34, 65, 70, 138, 184
Erikson, E., 147
Essenes, 48
Evans-Wentz, W. Y., 86, 153

"False satori," 90
Fana, 61, 107
Feeling *(vedana)*, 121
Ferguson, P., 179
Flow, 181–184
Formless contemplations as meditation subjects, 8, 17–19
"Fourth Way," 92–97. *See also* Gurdjieff, George I.
Free association, 173
Freud, Sigmund, 140–141, 148, 154, 173
Fromm, Erich, 156
Full absorption. *See* Jhanas

Garfield, C., 179
"God consciousness," 70–71, 112
Goenka, S. N., 162–163
Goffman, E., 143
Goleman, D., 79, 168
Gowan, J., 179
Great fixation, 107
Greed *(lobha)*, 123, 124, 125
Gurdjieff, George I., 103, 106, 166
  "Fourth Way" of, 92–97
Gurdjieffian technique, 166–168
  self-remembering exercise, 95
Guru, 109
  role, in Hindu Bhakti, 43

Tantric yoga and, 80
Tibetan lama as, 87
Gyana yoga, 72

Hal (states reached by purification), 60
Halevi, Z'ev ben Shimon, 48, 49, 50, 51
Hare, 41
Hartmann, E., 182
Harvard Business Review, 165
Hateful persons, 129, 130–131
Headaches, 168
Heart disease, 170
Hesse, Herman, 153
Hesychasm, 52–58, 103
Hesychius of Jerusalem, 55
"Hinayana" tradition, 82. *See also* Theravadan Buddhist meditation methods
Hindu Bhakti. *See* Bhakti
Hirai, T., 176
Hui Hai, 91
Hypertension, 168, 170, 180

I Ching, 153, 154
Ibn al-Najib, 62
Immune system, 170
Impartiality *(tatramajjhata)*, 124–125, 138
Impermanence *(anicca)*, 25, 32
Indian Tantra yoga. *See* Tantra yoga
Infinite awareness, 18
Infinite space, 18
Inflexibility, 147–148
Inquisition, 143
Insight *(panna)*, 123
Insight, path of, 3, 20
  cessation of consciousness and, 36–38
  effortless insight state, 29–30
  first realizations of, 23, 25–26

Insight *(continued)*
  higher realizations and, 27–28
  landmarks on, 24
  Mahayana tradition and, 83
  mindfulness and, 20–23, 110
  nirvanic state, 30–36
  and path of concentration,
    37
  perceptions on, 27–29
  pseudonirvana stage, 26–27
  psychoanalytic view of,
    148–150
  self-remembering and, 95
  Visuddhimagga on, 20–38
Introspection, 118
Introspectionists, 146
Introversion, 57–58
Ischemia, 170
Isherwood, C., 71
Ishta. See Devotional object

James, William, 141, 145, 151
Japa (repetition of the name),
    42, 44, 46, 80
Japanese Zen. *See* Zen
Jewish Kabbalah. *See* Kabbalah
Jhanas (full absorption), 104,
    107, 175
  altered states of consciousness
    and, 111
  Bhakti and, 44–45
  described, 13
  eighth level, 18–19, 36, 37
  fifth, 17–18
  first, 13
  formless, 17, 37
  fourth, 16–17
  key attributes of, 110
  levels of, 144
  meditation subjects and, 19
  mindfulness and, 21–22
  one-pointedness and, 14
  personality and, 137

second, 14, 16, 18
seventh level, 37
sixth, 18
speed of traversing, 19
stages of, 13–19, 144
Tibetan Buddhism and, 84–85
Transcendental Meditation
    and, 67
Jivan-mukti (liberated man), 75,
    76
Johansson, Rune, 137–138
John of the Cross, St., 151
Joriki, 89
Joshua ben Miriam, 48
*Journal of Transpersonal
    Psychology,* 159–160
Journey to the East (Hesse), 153
Jung, Carl, 138, 153–156, 158

Kabbalah, 48–52, 78, 103, 108
  cosmology of, 48–49
  meditation in, 50–52
Kabir, 47–48
Kadloubovsky, E., 54, 55
Kalisantaram Upanaishad, 41
Kapala (cup from human skull),
    79–80
Kapleau, P., 90
Karma, 120, 144
Karma yoga, 72
Kasamatsu, A., 176
Kasinas, as meditation subjects,
    8, 12, 17
Kavvanah, 51
Kensho-godo, 89
Keung, P., 179
Kiecolt-Glaser, Janice, 170
Kirtan (chanting and singing),
    41, 80
Koan, 88–89, 90
Krishna, Lord, 41
Krishnamurti, J., 97–101,
    103–104, 105, 107

Ku (empty or voidness), 91
Kundalini yoga, 77–82, 108
  chakras, 77, 78
Kyrie eleison, 54

Lao Tzu, 38
Lesh, T. V., 179
"Lesser Vehicle," 82. *See also*
  Theravadan Buddhist
  meditation methods
Levitation, 71
Loving kindness *(karuna),* 131,
  138
Luckmann, T., 108
Lustful persons, 131

Macarius, 53
Maggid (teacher), 50, 51
Mahabba, 61
Mahamudra, 86
Maharishi Mahesh Yogi, 66, 68,
  70–71
"Mahayana" tradition, 82–87,
  104
Maithuna (arousal of kundalini
  energy through ritual
  sexual intercourse), 78–79
Makyo (visions and intense
  sensations), 90
Mala (rosary), 42
Mandalas, 154
Mantra, 41, 67–68, 78, 79, 80,
  98, 186–187
Martial arts, 167–168
Maslow, Abraham, 147, 156,
  158–159
Mazkur (one remembered), 61
Meditation. *See also* Meditation
  paths
  effects on brain, 165–166
  flow and, 181–184
  how to, 185–189
  NIH report and, 168

norepinephrine and, 170
  as path to mental health,
    133–137
  practices and applications,
    185–189
  psychology of, 114–189
  recovery from stress and,
    164
  relaxation versus, 169
  research on, 163–165,
    175–181
  stress and, 162–165
Meditation paths. *See also*
    specific meditation systems
  goal of, 112
  Kaballists and, 50–52
  Krishnamurti and, 98–99
  personality types and,
    129–131
  psychoanalytic view, 148–150
  retraining attention,
    comparison of techniques
    for, 104–107
  similarities and differences,
    39–40, 53, 61, 62, 63, 67,
    72–73, 82–83, 87, 97,
    102–113, 177–178
  survey of, 39–101
  transformation of the self
    and, 115
  typology of, 105–107
Meditation subjects. *See also*
    Object of meditation
  formless contemplations as,
    17–19
  jhanic levels and, 13–19
  matching to temperament,
    8–9
  verge of absorption and,
    12
  Visuddhimagga on, 7–8
Melancholia, 148
Mental disorders, 131

Mental factors, 119–127
  healthy, 120–121, 123–126,
    131, 132, 133–134
  inhibition of, 13–14, 123–126
  neutral, 121
  patterns of, 127
  perceptual/cognitive, 126
  personality types and, 127
  unhealthy, 120–123, 126, 131,
    132, 133–134
Mental health, 131
  Allport and, 147
  anusayas and, 132
  criterion for, 131
  meditation as path to,
    133–137
Mental states
  chakras and, 77–78
  inflexible, 123
  influence on behavior,
    127–131
  mental health and, 131
  mindfulness of, 22
  neutral properties in, 121
  polar opposites, 123
  properties (*see* Mental
    factors)
  in relation to sense objects,
    118
Merton, Thomas, 53–54, 56, 92,
  184
Metabolism, 19, 36–37
Metatron, 48
Middle Ages, 143
Milarepa, 86
Mind, in relation to body, 125
Mind objects, 22–23
Mind reading, 82
Mindfulness *(sati)*, 20–23, 105,
  110, 123, 127, 175–176
  bare insight method and,.
    21–22
  of the body, 22

control of senses and, 4
detachment and, 174
eating and, 187–188
of feeling, 22
Gurdjieff and, 95
jhanas and, 21–22
kinds of, 22–23
maintaining, 136
meditation on breath and,
  187
of mental states, 22
of mind objects, 22–23
path of insight and, 110
perceptual abilities and, 135
research study, 176
self-remembering and, 94
Zen and, 91
Misdiscernment *(ditthi)*, 121–122
Mnemonic devices, 42
"Mobile zazen," 89
Modesty *(hiri)*, 124
Monks, 133
  Buddhist, 3, 4–5, 6, 21, 53,
    115
  Christian, 52–58, 104
  Hindu, 53
  research study, 176
Motivation, 127–128
Mudras (methods for cleansing
  internal organs), 73, 80
Muktananda, Swami, 80–81, 109
Muragaba (insight technique),
  107
Muscle control, and Gurdjieff
  training, 167–168

Nafs (habitual impulses), 64
Nanamoli Thera, 1
Narada, 41
National Institute of Health
  (NIH), 168, 170
Nibbana, 136–137. *See also*
  Nirvana

Nicholson, R. A., 61
Nidich, S., 179
Nilius, St., 56
Nirodh (cessation), 36–38
  metabolism and, 36, 37
Nirvana, 1, 20, 30, 110
  alteration of consciousness
    and, 30–36
  dreaming and, 34
  hinayana, 82
  levels of mastery, 31–36
  moment of penetration of, 30
  psychoanalytic view of, 149
  Western use of term, 144
Nirvikalpa samadhi, 75
Niyama, 73
No-thing-ness, 18, 37
Nonattachment *(alobha)*,
  124–125
Nonaversion *(adosa)*, 124–125
Nonexistence. See *Anatta*
Nonself. *See* Self
Norepinephrine, 170
Nyanaponika Thera, 21, 116
Nyanatiloka Mahathera, 122

Object of meditation, 10–11,
  14. *See also* Meditation
  subjects
"Objective consciousness," 96,
  97
"Observing I," 94
Oceanic feeling, 140
One-pointedness, 11, 13–14, 16,
  17, 18, 37, 67, 106, 110,
  175
  concentration and, 174
  on *ishna*, 42
  mindfulness and, 21
  as neutral property of mental
    state, 121
  Patanjali's ashtanga yoga and,
    72

Tibetan Buddhism and, 84
Transcendental Meditation
  and, 67
Orage, 92
Orme-Johnson, D. W., 179
Ornish, Dean, 170
Ouspensky, P. D., 92, 93, 94, 95

Pain, 16, 171
Pali, 20, 87, 120, 145, 148
Pali Canon, 115
Palmer, G. E. H., 54, 55
Patanjali, 71, 151. *See also*
  Ashtanga yoga system
Patel, Chandra, 170
Pelletier, K., 178, 179
Perception(s), 18, 46, 121, 135
  clarity of, 184
  dual, of *arahat*, 35
  on path to insight, 27–29
  sharpening of, 178, 183
  of Yaqui Indians, 144
Perplexity *(vicikiccha)*, 122
Personality, 178–179
  Abhidhamma on, 179
  of *arahat*, 137–138
  Buddhist psychology of,
    116–119
  meditation conditions and,
    129–131
  meditative subjects and, 8–9
  mental factors and, 127
  motivation and, 128
  nirvana and, 37
  tests of, 180
  types, 128–131
  Visuddhimagga on, 128–131
  Zen and, 92
Philokalia, 55, 56
Physical elements as meditation
  subjects, 8
Plotinus, 150–151
Poddar, H. P., 42, 44

Possessions, limitation of, 4–5
Prabhavananda, Swami, 71
Practices, 185–189
    mantras, 186–187
    meditation on the breath,
        185–186
    mindful eating, 187–188
    mindful walking, 189
Pranayam (exercise to control
    breathing), 73, 78, 80
Pratyahara (fifth limb of
    ashtanga yoga), 74
Prayer, Christian, 53–54, 56
Prayer of Jesus, 55
Prayer of the Publican, 58
Preparation for meditation
    ashtanga yoga and, 72–74
    Bhakti and, 42–44, 103
    comparison among systems,
        102–104
    Hesychasm and, 53–57, 103
    Kabbalah and, 49–51, 103
    kundalini yoga and, 80–81
    Sufism and, 59–60, 62–63,
        103
    Tibetan Buddhism and, 84–85
    Transcendental Meditation
        and, 67–68
    Visuddhimagga and, 2–10
    Zen and, 88–91
Priests, 115
Principles of Psychology (James),
    145
Pseudonirvana, 26–27, 90
Psychic energy *(jivitindriya)*,
    121
Psychoanalysis, 140–141, 144,
    148, 157
Psychological testing, 178, 180
Psychologies. *See* Buddhist
    psychology; Eastern
    psychology; Western
    psychology

Psychology of Nirvana, The
    (Johansson), 137
Psychosomatic disorders, 164
Psychosynthesis, 157
Psychotherapy, 171–174
Psychotherapy, East and West
    (Watts), 158
Pulse, gearing recitation to, 42
Puñña. See Insight, path of
Purification
    Bhakti and, 42
    comparison of systems'
        requirements for, 102–103
    Hesychasm and, 56, 57–58
    kundalini yoga and, 80
    psychoanalysis and, 157
    Sufi path, 60
    Transcendental Meditation
        and, 68
    in *Visuddhimagga* tradition,
        2–9, 112
    yoga and, 73

Qurb, 61

Raja yoga, 73, 108
Rama, 41
Ramakrishna, Sri, 41, 46, 75,
    140
Ramana Maharshi, 43, 76, 108
Ramanujan, C. K., 143
Rapture, 13, 16
Reality, perception of
    arahat's, 33, 35
    culture and, 142–145
    Kabbalistic, 48–49
Receptivity, 20
"Reciprocal inhibition," 123,
    133–134
Recollection, 57
Rectitude *(cittujjukata),* 124
Reflections as meditation
    subjects, 7

Reich, Wilhelm, 147
Relaxation response, 186
Relaxation Response, The
(Benson), 169
Relaxation techniques, 169–172
Religion, Western, 139–142
*Religions, Values, and
Peak-experiences* (Maslow),
159
Remorselessness *(anottoppa)*, 122,
124
Research studies, 174–181
Respiration as meditation
subject, 12
Rigidity. *See* Inflexibility
Rinzai sect of Zen, 88
Rolland, Romain, 140
Rorschach test, 178
Rosary *(mala)*, 42, 53
Rudi, 108
Rudrananda, Swami, 108–109
Rules for Monasteries, 58

Sadhana, 82
Sahaj samadhi, 46–47, 76
Suhusrara (topmost chakra),
81
Saints, 108, 113, 116
arahat as, 139
Saiva Upanishads, 67
Sakadgami (once returner),
32–33
Samadhi. See Concentration,
path of
Samsara, 82
Samyama, 74
Sangha, 5, 83
Sankaracharya, 45, 66–67
Sanskrit, 67–68, 146
Saradananda, Swami, 45–46
Sati. See Mindfulness
Satori awakening, 89, 91–92
Satprem, 109

Satsang (company of people of
same path), 42
Savichara samadhi. See Access
concentration
Schiller, J., 140–141
Schizophrenia, 171
catatonic, 148–149
Scholem, G., 52
Schuman, Marjorie, 175
Schwartz, Gary E., 163, 168,
179
Secret Garden, The (Shabastri),
63–64
Seeman, W., 179
Self
Abhidhamma on, 117–118
acceptance of, 179
Allport's view of, 147
awakened states and, 112
Bhakti and, 43, 47
Buddhist psychology and,
122, 147
Gurdjieff and, 95–96
Hesychasm on, 56–57
hinayana nirvana and, 82
Kabbalist view, 52
Krishnamurti on, 100
realization of nonexistence of
(anatta), 24, 25–26, 33, 35
sahaj samadhi and, 76
surrendering, 9
transformation of, 115
Zen and, 91
Self-actualization, 47, 158
"Self-knowledge," 99–100, 106
Self-observation, 94–95
"Self-remembering," 94–95, 106
Selye, Hans, 172
Senoi, 144
Senses, control of, 4
Sensual persons, 128–129, 130
Settings for meditation,
spectrum of, 103–104

Sexual activity, 33, 78–79, 118–119
Sexual thoughts, 3–4
Shabastri, Mahmud, 63–64
Shabd (supersubtle inner sounds), 78
Shah, Idries, 62, 65–66
Shakti (kundalini energy), 78
Shaktipat diksha, 80–81, 111
Shamelessness *(ahirika),* 122
Shapiro, Deane, 168, 175
Shat-karmas (methods for cleansing internal organs), 73
Shikan-taza (just sitting), 106
Shiney, 83. *See also* Concentration, path of
Shunyata (direct experience without any props), 86
Siddha yoga, 80
Siddhartha (Hesse), 153
Siddhis (supernormal psychic powers), 81–82, 86
Sila (virtue or moral purity), 2, 83
Simeon the Stylite, St., 54
Singing and chanting, 41, 80
Sotupanna (stream enterer), 32
Spillover, 182
Srimad Bhagavatam, 41, 44
Stress, 162–165, 169–172
Sublime states as meditation subjects, 7, 8
Suffering, 26, 93, 121–122
Sufi Rule for Novices, A (Abu al-Najib), 62
Sufism, 59–66, 103, 107, 108, 111
Sunyata, 85
Surwit, Richard, 171
Sutich, Anthony, 159–160
Suzuki, D. T., 35, 88, 90, 153, 156

Symbols, in dreams, 138
Synchronicity, 138

Talmud, 51
Tantra yoga, 77–82
Tantrics of the Bon Marg, 79, 103
Tao Te Ching (Lao Tzu), 39
Tart, Charles, 111, 160–161
Teacher, 9–10. *See also* Guru; *Maggid*
  Krishnamurti on, 104
  Sufism and, 62, 63
Telepathy, 74
Temperament. *See* Personality
"Ten Corruptions of Insight," 26–27
Theory Z, 158, 159
Theravadan Buddhist meditation methods, 2–38, 52, 82, 87, 105–106, 108, 115, 177
Thoreau, Henry David, 151
Tibetan(s)
  kapala, 79–80
  two levels of religion, 39
Tibetan Book of the Dead, The, 153
Tibetan Book of the Great Liberation, The, 153
Tibetan Buddhism, 82–87
Tiferet (state of heightened awareness), 49, 51
Titchener, E. B., 146
TM. *See* Transcendental Meditation
Torah, 52
Torpor *(middha),* 123
Traits of consciousness, altered, 175, 177–181
Trance, 155, 175
"Transcendental consciousness," 68, 69, 107, 112

Transcendental Meditation
(TM), 66–71, 103, 106,
107, 108, 150, 166–168
Transcendentalists, 151
Transformations of Consciousness,
162
Transpersonal psychologies,
160–161
Transpersonal Psychologies (Tart,
ed.), 160
"Triple Refuge," 83
Turiya (absorption), 81, 107
Turiyatita, 81

Unconscious, 118, 173
"Unity," in Transcendental
Meditation, 71, 112
Unselfishness, 33–34

Vajiranana, P., 128
Vajrayana, 86
Van Aung, Z., 118
Varieties of Religious Experience
(James), 151
Vedantic philosophy, 152
Verbal thoughts, 14
Vipassana, 85, 88, 90, 95. *See
also* Insight, path of
Virtue, 2, 43–44. *See also*
Purification
Vishnu, 41
Visions, 12–13, 109. *See also*
Mayko
Visualization, 83–84, 85
Visuddhimagga (Buddhaghosa),
1–38, 40, 42, 54, 63, 72,
82. *See also Abhidhamma*
on attention retraining,
104
on entry into awakened
states, 113
on meditation conditions for
personality types, 129–131

on meditative subjects, 7–8
on path of concentration,
10–19
on path of insight, 20–38
on personality types, 128–131
on preparation for
meditation, 2–10
purification process and, 2–9,
112
typology of meditation
techniques, 105–107
Zen and, 87, 89
Vivekananda, Swami, 43–44, 71,
151
Vocabulary, and culture and,
142, 144
Void, as object of meditation,
18
Volition *(cetana),* 121
Vyas Dev, Swami, 73

Wadis, 97
Walad, Sultan, 59
Walker, Kenneth, 93–94, 95–
96
Walking, mindful, 189
Walsh, R., 168
Watson, J. B., 146
Watts, Alan, 157–158
Wei Wu Wei, 35
Western psychology, 114, 115,
116, 120, 122, 139–162
altered states of consciousness
and, 139–145
awareness of Eastern
psychology, 145–147
commonalities with Eastern
psychology, 147–150
dissemination of Eastern
psychological theories to,
150–162
worldview, 139–142
Whitman, Walt, 151, 152

Wilber, Ken, 162
Wilhelm, Richard, 153
"Witness," 94
World Congress of Religions,
First, 151
Worry *(kukkucca),* 122–123,
131, 169

Yama, 73
Yantra (objects for visualization
exercises), 78
Yaqui Indians, 144
Yasutani, 88–89, 90
Yesod (ego), 49, 51

Yoga, 155, 171
ashtanga, 71–76
kundalini, 77–82, 105, 107,
108
Yoga Sutras (Patanjali), 151
Yogi, 75, 76, 86, 115

Zakir (one who remembers), 61
Zazen, 87–92, 104–105
Zen, 87–92, 103, 104, 108, 150,
176, 177
Zenrim, 10
Zikr (remembrance), 59, 107
Zimmer, Heinrich, 153